Series No. 8

SCRIPTIONS OF ANDHRA PRAD

KARIMNAGAR DISTRICT

Edited by

Sri P. V. Parabrahma Sastry, M.A.

Deputy, Director (Epigraphy)

Department of Archaeology and Museums, A. P., Hyderabad.

General Editor

Dr. N. RAMESAN, M. A., Ph. D., I. A. S.,

Director of Archaeology and Museums,

and Member, Board of Revenue,

Government of Andhra Pradesh, Hyderabad.

Published by

THE GOVERNMENT OF ANDHRA PRADESH

Rs. 53/-

PRINTED AT
THE ANDHRA PRADESH GOVT. TEXT-BOOK PRESS
MINT COMPOUND, HYDERABAD
ANDHRA PRADESH.

PREFACE

The present book on Karimnagar inscriptions is the second volume in the eries of the exhaustive list of inscriptions of Andhra Pradesh which the department f Archaeology has undertaken to bring out, the first volume being the inscriptions f Warangal district. The contiguity of Karimnagar district to Warangal District ; so close, that for purposes of archaeological analysis the region as a whole could e viewed as a single unit.

The history of Warangal region from its inscriptions is known from the rise f the Kākatīyas in the middle of twelfth century A. D., whereas Karimnagar egion by virtue of its proximity to the river Godavari, has yielded greater results f antiquarian importance. Its antiquity dates back to the early dim phases of he dawn of history, which is attested to by the cave dwellings noticed on a hillock ear Kapparaopet, popularly known as *munula-gutta*, the hill of ascetics, on the ight bank of Godavari where some microliths, Śātavāhana coins and some early aina vestiges were discovered during the recent exploration work. Pedabankur n the same Peddapalli taluk, as a result of archaeological excavations has proved tself to be a very important Śātavāhana site in Andhra Pradesh.

The next phase in the historical period of the region begins with the eign of the Chalukya collateral branch called the Vēmulavāda Chālukyas, whose istory started simultaneously with the advent of the Rāshṭrakūṭa power. Vinayā-litya Yuddhamalla, the founder of the family ruled over the *Sapādalaksha* country vith Podana, modern Bodhan as his capital, in the ninth century A. D. and his ingdom extended upto Chennuru near Manthena on the river Godavari. Later Arikēsari II (A.D. 930-955) shifted the capital to Vēmulavāḍa. It would appear hat subsequent to the fall of the Rāshṭrakūṭa power, their successors, the Western Chālukyas bestowed this region, known as Sabbi-nāḍu, on the early Kākatīya hiefs. The Vēmulavāḍa Chālukyas patronized Jainism and built several temples o Jain *Tīrthaṅkaras* at places like Vēmulavāda, Sanigaram, Nagunuru and Gaṅgā-lharam. The most notable event of the reign of those kings was, that the great Kannada poet Pampa and the Jain theologist Sōmadēva-sūri flourished in their royal ourt. The monumental works Vikramārjuna-Vijaya, Ādipurāṇa, Yaśastilaka and Nītivākyāmṛita were produced during the reign of these kings and made their names mmortal. Other chiefs like Mēḍarāja of Polavasa, his brother Guṇḍarāja of Man-thena, Dommarāja of Naganuru and Ēḍarāja of Ramagundam appear as enemies of the Kākatīyas and were vanquished by them.

About eighty inscriptions in all were copied in this district and they are edited here by Sri P. V. P. Sastry, Deputy Director (Epigraphy). Most of the part in the district were surveyed by Sri M. V. N. Aditya Sarma, Assistant Directo

(Epigraphy), Sri T. Mallikarjunarao and Sri G. Chandraiah, Epigraphy Assistants in addition to other members of the epigraphy staff. I am grateful to all these my assistants for their active co-operation. My thanks are also due to Sri B.V. Reddy, Director of Government Text-book Press, Sri G. Ramakrishna Rao, Deputy Director (Technical), Sri V. Gangadharam and other staff of the press who got this publication through the press in time.

N. RAMESAN

HYDERABAD
Dated: 11-10-1974.

CONTENTS

gapuram	Inscription of Western	Chālukya	Bhūlōkamalladēva
garam	,,	,,	Jagadēkamalladēva
ımnagar	,,	Kākatīya	Rudradēva
laram	,,	,,	,,
iella	,,	,,	[Mahādēva ?]
ıthena	,,	,,	Gaṇapatidēva
ıkuru	,,	,,	,,
lisala (Upparapally)	,,	,,	,,
.rmapuri	,,	,,	,,
esvaram	,,	,,	,,
laram	,,	,,	,,
mmampalli	,,	,,	,,
ıgal	,,	,,	Rudradēva
ıabad	,,	,,	Rudradēva
;edu	,,	,,	Pratāparudradēva
:tapur	,,	,,	,,
onda	,,	,,	,,
visomanapalli	,,		(Miscellaneous)
visomanapalli	,,		,,
ıvasa	,,		,,
ısagar	,,		,,
igaram	,,	Velama Chiefs	
esvaram	,,	Vijayanagara	Dēvarāya
ıntagiri	,,	,,	(Miscellaneous)
ıagiri Fort	,,	,,	,,
lulla	,,	Velama Chiefs	
ırmapuri	,,	,,	Jāpalli Dharmarāya

dipalli	Inscription	(Miscellaneous)
ulla	,,	,,
nipaḷem	,,	,,
llannapet	,,	of Velama Chiefs
igaram	,,	of Sultān Abdulla Kutubshāh
illa	,,	(Miscellaneous)
gunuru	,,	,,
nalapur	,,	,,
dipalli	,,	,,
dipalli	,,	,,
ipeta	,,	,,
irājupalli	,,	,,
apur	,,	,,
ulavāda	,,	,,
nbhirpur	,,	,,
shanraopet	,,	,,
asa	,,	,,
illa	,,	,,
kal	,,	,,
tapagirikota	,,	,,
esvaram	,,	,,
esvaram	,,	,,
thakunta	,,	,,
thakunta	,,	,,
gunuru	,,	,,
asa	,,	of Mēḍarāja

HISTORICAL INTRODUCTION

THE CHĀLUKYAS OF VĒMULAVĀḌA

ıe known history of this district begins with the line of kings called the Chālukyas c mulavāḍa, who flourished as subordinates of considerable prominence under the Rā ıt they continued right from the rise of theRāshṭrakūṭa power till its downfall in A y of chiefs in the entire Telingāṇa region was politically so great as the family of t ıkyas during that period. Scholars generally believe that Vēmulavāḍa which is a from Karimnagar was their capital; but there are some indications that Bodhan o ıbad district was their original capital and later shifted to Vēmulavāḍa. Two set ptions namely the Kollipara plates of Arikēsari I and the Parabhani plates of Arikē a epigraph of Arikēśari II and the Kānnaḍa literary work *Vikramārjuna-vijaya* pa form the main source material in constructing the history of these kings. Thes es have been thoroughly discussed by Dr. N. Venkataramanayya in his monograph *(V)ēmulavāḍa*' published by the Archaeological Department, Government of Hyc ıronological table of these chiefs is given in it as follows.

Chālukya family		
ıditya Yuddhamalla I	...	750-775 A.D.
ıari I	...	775-800 "
ṁha I	...	800-825 "
ıamalla II	...	825-850 "
ga	...	850-895 "
ıamalla III	...	895-915 "
ṁha II	...	915-930 "
ıari II	...	930-955 "
āja	...	955-965 "
ıari III	...	966 ... ...

is most unfortunate to note that the present epigrāphical survey in the region did r ts which may help us in formulating a more precise chronological scheme than that

he region, according to the inscriptions is known as *Sapādalaksha*, that is, consi urth lakh villages or revenue divisions. The earliest reference in this context is n ḍa inscription of Arikēsari II which states that Vinyāditya-Yuddhamalla, the found lukya Chiefs ruled *Sapādalaksha* with Pōdana as his capital town. Two more inscr lace, one belonging to Baddega of the same family, another to Rājāditya, a sul n Chālukyas mention the region as *Sapādalaksha*. The view of the early writers th *sha* in those days was applicable only to Kanuja, Nepal, Kalinga, Kēdāra, Kāsm nkaṇa but not to any part of the Telugu country, is not acceptable.[1] Their argum he list of *Sapādalaksha* regions given in the Telugu work *Paṇḍitārādhya-charit* Sōmanātha.[2] Two of the above mentioned places namely Kēdāra and Tirk

---

N.Venkataramanayya: *The Chālukyas of Vēmulavāḍa* - p. 15

ḍitārādhya - charitra; Parvata prakaraṇamu

ude or not the present Bōdhan-Vēmulavāḍa region in his list of *Sapādalaksha-deśas*[1]
er hand the three epigraphical evidences prove beyond the least trace of doubt th
on consisted of the present districts of Nizamabad and Karimnagar in Teling
śmanta, Sabbi-*nāḍu* twenty-one thousand and other regions of the early per
a-Yuddhamalla when he first rose to fame by virtue of a victorious military exp
is Rāshṭrakūṭa overlord Dantidurga, gave the name of *Sapādaluksha* to his nat
a in the present Karimnagar district is not a reasonable proposition. *Sa*
la are not two different regions and their identity with Kōsala is worth suggestin

a, present Bōdhan in the Nizamabad district, was in all its probability the capital of Y
ling to the Vēmulavāḍa inscription of Arikesari II, casued his elephants to be bathed i
oil. The antiquity of this town goes to the early period of the Sātavāhanas as is ev
ad fort which resembles the fort at Dhanakaṭaka near Amarāvati. Koṇḍapur in the Me
nkur in the Karimnagar district as a result of the archaeological explorations, have eme
ites of the Sātavāhana period and it may not be improbable that Pōdana if explore
milar results. Sir Alexander Cunningham while tracing the course of the path t
g, states that the Chinese traveller, after crossing the borders of Kosala proce
intry where he visited its capital named *Ping-ki-lo*, which is at a distance of 900
Chanda, a town in Kosala according to him. He (Cunningham) locates *Ping-*
Karimnagar.[2] In such case, it would be more appropriate if, the place is identified w
ankur. The phonetic accent of *Ping-ki-lo* very conveniently applies to Bankur.
aph from Chennur on the northern bank of the Godavari in the Adilabad district
Pōdana-*nāḍu* even in the days of Arikēsari II.[3] It seems thus, quite reasonable
a was the original capital of these Chālukya chiefs who subsequently by the time of A
ier shifted their seat to Vēmulavāḍa. The Parbhani plates of Arikēsari IV, son of
ecord a grant of a village named Vanikaṭupulu to the great Jain scholar Sōm
eep of Śubhadhāma-*Jinālaya* built by Baddega in the capital Lēmbulapāṭaka.
the change of the capital from Pōdana to Lēmbulapāṭaka. Now, the question which
situated in *Sapādalaksha*, remains. The above mentioned Parbhani plates specificall
in that region. About the latter, the Vēmulavaḍa epigraph (No. 4) states th
Sapādalaksha, constructed a *Jinālaya* for Sōmadēva, the chief of the Gauḍa-*sam*
concluded that both Pōdana and Lēmbulavāṭika were included in the said region
his region, *Aśmaka* is stated by Sōmadēva which is identified with a hill
to Parbhaṇi plates also Yuddhamalla ruled over the *Sapādalaksha* country and
be bathed in a tank filled with oil at Pōdana.[5] From the foregoing discuss

---

Chālukyas of Vēmulavāḍa. p. 15, f.n.
nningham *"The Ancient Geography of India"* pp. 444. (published by Indological
nasi-1963.)
Annual Report on Epigraphy 1967, No. 320.
antaka-vēśma vihāya yāhi" Yaśastilaka champu Book III. Śṛitasāgara, the commentator explains
dalaksha mountain, which is identified with the Barbora hill in Bērar. The capital of Aśmaka
=āditya-bhavō-vamśaś Chālukya iti viśrutaḥ-tatr=ābhūd Yuddhamall-ākhyō nṛipatir=vikrama-[illegible]
a-bhū - bhartā taila-vāpyāṁ sa Pōdane avagāh-ōtsavaṁ chakrē Śakraśrīr=[illegible]" Th
Vēmulavāḍa, p. 94.

le to assume that these Chālukya chiefs were holding their principality in the regio
ia to Chennūr along the river Godavari even from the time of Yuddhamalla.

ayāditya-Yuddhamalla was succeeded by his son Arikēsari I and he is supposed to
ility in the last quarter of the eighth century A.D. According to the Kollipara
been proficient in several branches of learning like grammar, law, *gajatantra*, m
he plates were issued by the king to register the gift to the Śaiva ascetic named M
Sadyśśivāchārya, of a village Aṁkuṭa (?) as *vidyādāna*. The date of the record
21, that is A.D. 1019, does not tally with the assumed period of the king. Thi
ns regarding the genealogy, lead us to suspect the genuineness of the record.[1] An
's period is the Kuravagaṭṭa epigraph which simply states some exploits of his youn
who was a friend of Gōvindavallabha son of Kalivallabha, that is Rāshṭrakūṭa ki
'93). Gōvindavallabha is obviously Gōvinda III (A.D. 793-814).

ext important king among these chiefs was Baddega (A.D.850-895) the son of Yud
the title *Soluda-Gaṇḍa* (the unvanquished hero); he was a great warrior and d
have fought forty-two battles. Accroding to the Vēmulavāḍa inscription of Arikē
Vikramārjuna-vijaya, Baddega defeated Chālukya Bhīma identified with Bh
Guṇaga Vijayāditya and ruled Vēngi from A.D. 892 to 922. This must have
of the expeditions conducted by his overlord Rāshṭrakūṭa Kṛishṇa II on Vēngi.

uddhamalla III succeeded Baddega. Narasiṁha II his son and successor was
dited with several military adventures. He conquered the Latas, the Malavas, M
Gurjaras, caused his horses to bathe in the river Gaṅgā and set up a stone pilla
a; all of these victories being achieved on behalf of the Rāshṭrakūṭa king Indr
buted with the same victories in the Cambay plates of his son and successor Gōvind
ef that Narasiṁha II had marital relation with the Rāshṭrakūṭa royal family by havin
va as his queen is not inconceivable. Paṁpa's statement[3] that Arikēsarin II, as
ulder as his cradle is suggestive of such relation between the two families.
II participated in all the military exploits of Indra III and appro
his credit.

e present collection begins with the Inscriptions of Arikēsarin II who succeede
II in about A.D. 930. Not only being the son of the Rāshṭrakūṭa princess Jākavva
mādi, the daughter of Indra III and Lōkāṁbikā another princess of the same roya
erefore with the Rāshṭrakūṭa kings was more intimate than that of his father. His p
entful and illustrious in more than one aspect. His Vēmulavāḍa inscription (N
ome of his creditable deeds. A more detailed account of them is given in *Vikrama*
to have given asylum at his court to certain Bijja of the Chālukya lineage. He defe
anta, whom Gojjiga sent against him at the head of an army. He assisted Baddega
Rāshṭrakūṭa throne. Of all the events mentioned here, the dethronement of Gōvi
le achievement of Arikēsarin II.

Chālukyas of Vēmulavāḍa p. 75.
VII No. 6.
mārjuna-vijayaṁ, I. 44.

ijja or Bijayita to whom Arikēsarin gave asylum was undoubtedly the Chālukya .a family who had a principality lying beyond the south-eastern border of the \ 'he Mogalicheruvu grant of Kusumāyudha IV[1] and the Koravi epigraph of Niravad records of these chiefs. According to the brief historical account of that family i record their genealogical table can be constructed as follows.

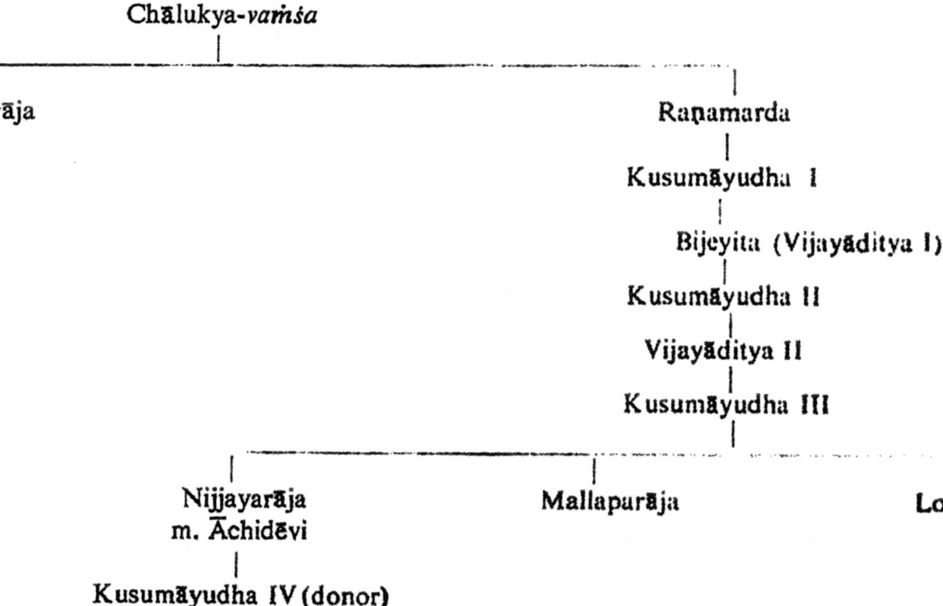

ie original plates are not available at present and neither the facsimile nor any copy c by its editor. Thus we are at a loss to deduce a better rendering of the text than w r whose reading is not altogether reliable. Even after making some reasonable xist serious doubts in the above table. For the present it is our concern which s shown in the table sought asylum in the court of Arikēsarin II. The possibil ' another Vijayāditya, though not mentioned in the Mogalicheruvu grant cannot b vi epigraph which narrates some important political events of these chiefs le in its language as well as contents and still complicates the identification of Bijja ulavāḍa inscription of Arikēsarin II and Paṁpa's *Vikramārjuna-vijaya*. For, i entions two sons of certain Kusumāyudha namely Goṇaga and his younger brother this record is identical with Bijja or Bijayita who took asylum in Arikēsarin's c er confirmed by the recently discovered Chennur epigraph[3] with a date equal to records a gift of land by Chālukya Goṇagarasa's son Baddega who is stated to be kēsariṇ. But quite disappointingly the names of Niravadya and his nephew Badd e Mogalicheruvu grant in association with either of the two personages named Vijay jayāditya. Surprisingly enough, another set of copper plates, also recently c

ı. XXXII pp. 281-84.
phia *Andhrica* I, pp. 118 ff.
. *R*. 1967, No. 320.
adhrica II, pp. 39 ff

rachalam furnishes a fresh list of some more chiefs of the same Chālukya family on may be linked with the table given above. It begins with a chief named Kari lished himself at Koravi. He was succeeded by his younger brother Nijja; s continued at Koravi. The discontinuity of Kariya Goṇaga's line at Koravi indicate cal pressure he was forced to flee from Koravi and seek asylum at neighbouring V r Nijjayita who succeeded him to the Koravi throne is given a place in the m icheruvu grant whereas Kariya Goṇaga who left Koravi to Vēmulavāḍa wa ing assumption is acceptable only when Niravadya of the Koravi epigraph can be id f the aforesaid two copper plate records. This, along with other objections ha: /here in detail. Summing up the discussion it may be tentatively accepted ' the Krivvaka grant, (Bhadrachalam plates) was the son of Kusumāyudha III of ant and he was identical with Bijja or Bijayita who took asylum in the court of A ximate date of this event is A.D. 934-5, corresponding to the date of Chālukya o the throne of Vēngi and the overthrowing of Gōvinda IV from the Rāshṭrakūṭa

was the rival kings of the neighbouring states and the dissatisfied subordinates acy to oust Gōvinda and bring his uncle Amōghavarsha III to the throne. The pa II in this affair was of considerable diplomatic skill. Disregarding the relati V whose sister or half-sister he had married, Arikēsarin for reasons unknown, e to Amōghavarsha III or Baddega in ousting Gōvinda from the Rāshṭrak a another queen of Arikēsarin II might have been a daughter of Baddega Amōgl be noted that the Eastern Chālukya king Bhīma II was in enmity with Gōvinda I sarin II. He was just asserting his power in the Vēngi kingdom which was years by Yuddhamalla II, son of Tāḍa I. In this troubled situation in Vēngi, garasa, as it seems, although owed his allegiance to Chālukya Bhīma I in the he same loyalty to Yuddhamalla who usurped the kingdom. Gōvinda IV, the ma r became furious and marched his armies over the small principality of Koravi. n Koravi Goṇaga did not think of going to the court of Bhīma II, the new king o the assumption that during the period of uncertainty and unlawful occupation o lla II, Goṇaga availed himself of the opportunity in becoming independent. Even af accession to the Vēngi throne he continued perhaps as an independent chief. Or, it n at Bhīma II disregarding the claims of Amma I's son Bhīma the rightful h of Vēngi, was not acknowledged as his overlord by Goṇaga. His brother Niravadya Bhīma II and took shelter in Vēngi. Goṇaga, on the other hand had to face the nda IV but also Chālukya Bhīma II who ultimately won the kingdom of Vēngi. ess he fled to Vēmulavāḍa and sought asylum from Arikēsarin II. It is not u · Niravadya on behalf of his master Bhīma II was also instrumental in driving out C he language of the Koravi epigraph makes us believe the same course of events wh by the evidence of the Chennur epigraph stating that Baddega son of Chālukya me fief in the territory of Arikēsarin II. How Arikēsarin, in spite of his relatio ivinda IV still remains a mystery. Probably the immoral character and wicked won the kingdom through assassination of his brother Amōghavarsha II made him g the loyal subordinates and relatives who later joined hands with Baddega Amōgl 's help to Baddega is not mentioned in his Vēmulavaḍa inscription. Hen e incident of Baddega's capture of the Rāshṭrakūṭa throne might have taken plac this record.

kēsarin II was succeeded by his elder son Vāgarāja. Bhadradēva was another son of A ā. Vāgarāja was succeeded by Bhadradēva and the latter's son Arikēsarin III in order. small epigraph to have built Śubhadhāma-*jinālaya* for his preceptor Sōmadēvasūri, a-*saṁgha* (No. 4). Arikēsarin III issued the Parbhani plates to the same scholar r village *Kuttuṁvṛitti*-Vanikaṭupalu situated in Rēpāka-twelve in Sabbi-thousand for t e Śubhadhāma-*jinālaya* built by his father. According to Sōmadēva's *Yaśastilaka-c* arbhani plates, Leṁbulavāṭaka, the modern Vēmulavāḍa was the capital of the: mpleted his work, that is *Yaśastilaka-chaṁpu* in, the Śaka year 881 (expired). tl ddhārthi on *Madana-Trayōdaśi* of the month of Chaitra when Kṛishṇarāja was in his pāṭi after defeating the Pāṇḍya, Chōla, Chēra and others. He further states that he a place called Gangādhara in the kingdom of the Chālukya subordinate Vāgarāja. arin II. It is thus, evident that Sōmadēva completed his work in Ś. 881 or A.D. 9 gādhara which may be identified with the place where the Kurkyala epigraph of allabha is recently discovered on a hill called Bommala-guṭṭa (No. 3). It must ha ntre in those days.

e Vēmulavāḍa chiefs of the Chālukya lineage, though small in political status, chievements of immense literary value to their credit. Paṁpa's *Vikramārjuna-vijaya* npa-*Bhārata* in Kannaḍa and Sōmadēva's *Yaśastilaka* or *Yaśodhara-charita*, a *chaṁ* skrit are those two great works which were composed in the court of these Chāluk rahman by birth, Paṁpa lived in the court of Arikēsarin II. According to the Kurky younger brother Jinavallabha, their father and grandfather named Bhīmap ndra respectively were the natives of Vangipaṟṟu in Kamma-*nāḍu*. (the present Nar taluks) on the bank of the river Guṇḍlakamma and Jainas by faith. Paṁpa se king as a commander of the army. His *Vikramārjuna-vijaya* is the story of Mah *Ādipurāṇa* is a religious poem in which the story of the Jaina Tīrthaṁkaras was we find in epigraph No. 1, five verses from *Paṁpa-Bhārata*.[1]

other great scholar, who flourished under the patronage of these Chālukya cl *ri* a renowned theologian of the Jaina order. An inscription on the pedestal o the construction of Śubhadhāma-*jinālaya* by the king Baddega of the Chālukya lin head of Gauḍa-*saṁgha*. Baddega was the son of Arikēsarin II, by the Rāshṭrakūṭa 'Whether this prince ever ruled for any short period is much doubted, because uling till A.D. 959, the date of Sōmadēva's completing his work *Yaśastilaka*, and in plates were issued to Sōmadēva by Baddega's son Arikēsarin III. Sōmadēva's *Ya* of the prince Yaśōdhara son of Yaśōrgha the king of Ujjayini, a narration based ajor part of the book is devoted in describing the contemporary court life, polity, s of learning and philosophical doctrines. It is more or less an encycolpaedia on these e work being to preach the Jaina doctrines.

THE WESTERN CHĀLUKYAS

e kings in the present collection, are represented by nearly twenty epigraphs Choppadaṇḍi village is the earliest. It is dated Ś. 914 Nandana (A. D. 992) and rec lukya king Āhavamalla was ruling the kingdom, Iṟivabeḍeṅga Satyāśrayadēva's gift to the god Mārtāṇḍadēva of Choppadaṇḍi village. Another record (No. 9) of

ful to Dr. B. Ramachandra Rao, Reader Osmania University, who brought this to my notice.

king dated Ś. 917, Manmatha corresponding to A.D. 995 is copied from Jammikun lers of Anumakoṇḍa-*vishaya*. The importance of the record lies in stating that th malla, that is Taila II had successfully completed his northern campaign and defeated ictorious event of the king a local chief, who might have also participated in the of land to the god Āditya of that village Da(ja)mmikuṇṭa. Utpala was obviously kin who is also known as Muñja, Amōghavarsha and Śrīvallabha.[1] According to *Praba* śrutuṅga, many a battle took place between Vākpati II and Taila II. Perhaps this ter between the two kings in which the Mālwa king was finally taken as captive *ndhachintāmaṇi* states that the king Vākpati undertook his last expedition into inst the advice of his minister Rudrāditya. He was defeated after crossing the Gōd northern boundary of Tailapa's kingdom and was taken captive. He was finally ex lied in Ś. 919 or 997-98 A.D. his victory over Utpala mentioned in the present a which is dated Ś. 917 or 995 A.D. must be refering to the last decisive battle, b Thus the date of the death of Muñja-Vākpati can be precisely stated to be A.D.

scription No. 11 copied from the Śiva temple in the village Choppadaṇḍi, refers abeḍeṁga and records certain gift to the deity Divakēśvara by the king's *dādi*, akabba. Jayasiṁha II is represented by one of the Vēmulavāḍa epigraphs (No. 13) wh god Rājēśvara by Chikkarāja in Śaka year 955 or 1033 A.D. The Vēmulavāḍa ted C. V. 8, Rudhirōdgāri corresponding to A. D. 1083 records that Mahāma sa governing the region of Sabbi-twenty two thousands included in Kosavaḷa-*saval* Lēṁbulavāḍa installed the god Rājādityēśvaradēva and built a high temple for it. he king who was in his *nelavīḍu* at Kalyāṇa granted the gift of the village Sanl 0 for the worship of the god and maintaining a feeding house etc,. The gift was m e Śaiva ascetics belonging to the Bhujaṅgāvaḷi Kāḷāmukha sect. The present tem Vēmulavāḍa is generally believed to be the same which was constructed by nce of the same title is already noticed among the Vēmulavāḍa Chālukyas and in f the Rājēśvara temple itself in the Vēmulavāḍa inscription of Arikēsarin II (No. regarding the origin of the present Rājēśvara temple is a matter for reconsideration. l epithets of Rājādityarasa indicates his victorious campaigns over the Chōḷa coun the reign of Rājēndra Chōḷa. The epithets viz., *Toṇḍamaṇḍaḷika-maṇḍaḷ na, Kuniṁgila-kōṭāṭavī-dāvapāvaka, Rājēndra Chōḷa-kīrtivallī-pallava-nidāha-san ayarāya - vijaya-saṁharaṇa, Chōḷa-kaṭaka - sūṛakāra, Kāñchīpura-prabaḷa-ba* ire worth mentioning in this connection. Rājāditya's contemporaneity with the whose reign ended in A.D. 1043-4 is much doubtful. But he might have been in several Chālukya expeditions against the Chōlas conducted by Sōmēśvara I Kāñchi expedition in A.D. 1052-3 which brought credit to several subordinate the Chālukyas. The epithet *Vijayarāya-vijaya-saṁharaṇa* of Rājāditya in the pr that Rājēndra Chōḷa in the preceding epithet must be in all probability Rājēndr harge of the said battle after the death of his elder brother Vijayarāja *alias* R D. 1044-1054). Clearly, these epithets refer to the events taken place in the Ko sequent plundering of Kāñchi by Āhavamalla's armies. Mahāmaṇḍalēśvara Rāj n active member among the Chālukya generals right from the early fifties of the eleve

pp. 226-8.

ıave also plundered Toṇḍamaṇḍala and the Kuṇingala fort. The latter may be ide Koningal in the southern part of the Karṇāṭaka State.

e region comprising *Savalakke* and *Sabbi-nāḍu* was partly administered by appointed tya, Paramāra Jagaddēva (No. 19) and Kumāra Sōmēśvara (No. 20) with thei ḍa and partly by the feudal subordinates like the Kākatīyas and the members of the olavāsa. The present epigraphical survey in Warangal and Karimnagar districts ıe interesting records which furnish valuable information regarding the history of Bēta I, Prōla I, Bēta II and Prōla II have been represented by separate dated om Sanigaram village on the way to Karimnagar from Siddipet.

ıe earliest of them (No. 14) is dated in the Śaka year 973 and Vikṛti correspondi ing itself to the prosperous reign of Trailōkyamalladēva. His feudatory chief, *M* Bētarasa's minister Nāraṇayya son of Vaijarāja is stated to have renovated the dhamalla Jinālaya in Sanagara and with the consent of the local chiefs Muppa made the gift to the same, of a *rāṭaṇa* that is water-drawing pulley on a well. ıll in contents is much valuable in more than one respect. This is the only rec ignable to Kākatīya Bēta I. Secondly, it is next in order to the Mangallu gr ālukya king Dānārṇava [1] which makes a direct reference to the Kākatīyas. Thi rd. The Bayyaram tank inscription[2] of Kākati Mailāmbā, sister of Gaṇapatidē time a lengthy genealogy of these chiefs beginning from Venna, whose succ Guṇḍa II, Guṇḍa III, Eṟṟa and Piṇḍi Guṇḍa, Garuḍa Bēta, Prōla I, Tribhu s sons Rudra and Mahadēva and the latter's son Gaṇapatidēva. Excepting a sl mention of another Bēta as the son of Eṟṟa, the Mangallu charter gives the a and Guṇḍa who are identical with Guṇḍa III, Eṟṟa and Guṇḍa IV of the for he genealogical list furnished in the Bayyaram tank inscription Piṇḍi Guṇḍa or ıer of Garuḍāṅka Bēta or Bēta I. Between the Mangallu grant which was issued ıd the present Sanigaram epigraph of Bēta I dated Ś. 973 or A.D. 1051, there is ıe century. According to the convention of the historians it is a long duration sted between two generations. But the fact remains so. A passing remark in this f and unintelligible is found in the Telugu portion of the Gudur inscription of the āra Sōmēśvara dated C.V. 49 corresponding to A.D. 1124.[3] While eulogizing the chiefs there, it is stated that a lady of that family named Kāmavasāni took the ta of the Kākatīya family who was very young and restored his lost position l as a subordinate chief of the Emperor. That Garuḍa Bēta was quite young whe responsibility of his principality is clear from the above statement. Hence it m e to assume that the combined political career of both Guṇḍa IV and his son Bē 956 to 1052. The former at the time of the issue of the Mangallu charter that is A.D. ged twenty five years and the latter might have born in about A.D. 980 and The date of the present Sanigaram epigraph thus helps us in deciding the perio f the Kākatīya family.

Andhrica I, pp. 57-70.
pp. 71 ff.
us of Telingāṇa Inscriptions, Part 2, p. 78.

e second epigraph (No. 15) in the series belongs to Prōla I and it is dated in Śaka corresponding to A. D. 1053. With the usual Chālukya *praśasti*, mention was m ɔus reign of Trailōkyamalladēva. *Mahāsāmanta* Kākatīya Poḷalarasa is said to lential sites, a *rāṭaṇa* and some lands to the god Madhupēśvara installed by Madh ;anagara, on the occasion of a solar eclipse. In this case also this is the only kno o Prōla I. Secondly the date of the previous record that is, A.D. 1051 being ver present record, just within a short interval of less than two years, the last year of Bē of his son and successor Prōla I can be fixed more precisely within this short per rstwhile basing on other considerations. Prōla I in this record is stated to have a the *prasādu* or kindness of Trailōkyamalla. A similar statement can be noti rgah inscription of Tribhuvanamalla Durgarāja,[1] according to which Prōla got An ig with Sabbi-one thousand as permanent fief through a charter from Trailōkyama ēta I was enjoying might have been by an oral approval of the king. Some remarkabl have rendered to the king during the few years before the date of this record, that is rious deed must be of a military nature. There were some more chiefs whose reco tary exploits of the same period, particularly the events of Koppam battle and th Kāñchī. Prōla I also must have been one among those who participated in these t and won victory for his overlord Trailōkyamalla. Prōla I, thus started his caree f Anumakoṇḍa-*vishaya* into a larger territory including Sabbi-*nāḍu* one thousand o

ıc third inscription of the Sanigaram village belongs to Kākatīya Bēta II (No. 19 1022, Vyaya, Māgha śu. 15, Thursday, lunar eclipse is not verifiable according to Śaka year 1022 does not tally with Vyaya. However the week day and lunar ecl Māgha exactly coincide with each other in the given cyclic year Vyaya but the to January 10th of 1107 A.D. According to the Kazipet Dargah inscription of Du ken that Bēta II was alive upto only 1090 A.D. and his son Tribhuvanamalla iim some time before 1097 A.D. But the present epigraph proves beyond doubt D. 1107. Probably this might be one of his last years; for his son Prōla II's inscri temple inscription is dated A.D. 1117. With the present record it is possible to reduce n twentyfive years (A.D. 1090 to 1117), which remained unassignable to any particular . Another important feature in this record is the mention of Mahāmaṇḍalēśvara after the mention of Mahāmaṇḍalēśvara Bētarasa. The usual order of mentioni records is according to their superiority as well as official status. That being the cas ed in mentioning Bēta before the mention of Jagaddēva indicates that the latter wa the former in status. Besides, being a prince of the reputed Paramāra family, Jaga the emperor Tribhuvanamalla Vikramāditya VI and was enjoying preferential tre Some local politics might have altered the status between the two chiefs and consequ asserted his superiority over Jagaddēva. On account of this rivalry the latter se town of Anumakoṇḍa. Bēta's son Prōla II according to the narration of the ole inscription repulsed the enemy with all his might and saved the town.

ōla II is represented in the present collection by two epigraphs from the same nd 24). The former belongs to the reign of Bhūlōkamalladēva whereas the latter amalla II. The date of the latter is Ś. 1071, Śukla corresponding to A.D. 1149.

---

ous of Telingāṇa Ins., part 2, p. 25 ff.

of Prōla II named Repola Kuṟuvarasa is mentioned and his *daṇḍanāyaka* Maṇ *tra* and Kamma-*kula* is stated to have made some gifts of land and *rāṭaṇa* t a. The inscription is important in more than one aspect. One is, that Prōla II w ; secondly, he remained quite loyal to the Chālukya king till then; thirdly, the recc ıst one of not only Prōla II but also the early subordinate chiefs of the Kākatīya scription dated Ś. 1080 (A.D. 1158) of Rudrā in the Daksharamam temple[1] is kno ıignable to independent or semi-independent rule of Rudradēva. From this last rec e is absolutely no basis to suppose that the Kākatīyas revolted against their ov ing of Kalyāṇa and asserted independence.

ıother subordinate family prominently known in the district of Karimnagar during was that of Mēḍarāja and his descendants. Some epigraphs of these chiefs have c sampet taluk of Warangal district. The Medapalli epigraph[2] of Jaggadēva and t graph[3] of Guṇḍarāja, both in Narasampet taluk are very valuable in constructing ronology of these chiefs. Polavāsa on the right side of Gōdāvari in Karimnagar c for some time. The genealogy of these chiefs can be given as follows :

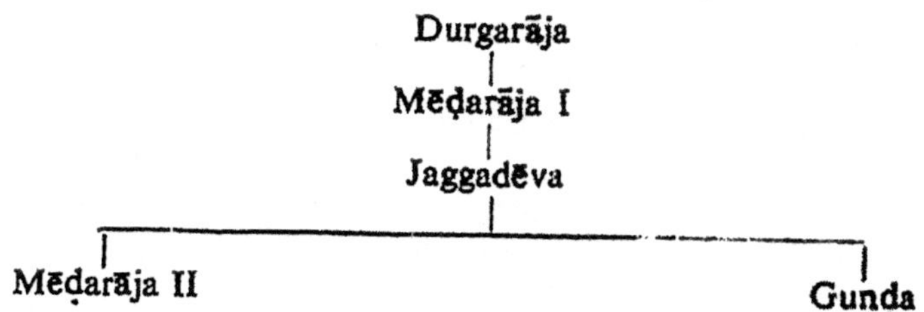

cording to the Gōvindapuram inscription they belong to the family of the mythical rman of Maṇināgapura who obtained royal fortunes by the grace of Yakshiṇi, a Jain ıe titles *Lattalūr-puravar-ādhīśvara, Śrī kēśavadēva-divya Śrī pāda-padmārādhaka* e ı Jainas in persuasion. We know little about the first member Durgarāja. Mēḍ ı the Polasa epigraph of A. D. 1108, as an independent chief. In the Banaji ēta II is mentioned as a donor of some gifts to Vīrakamaḷa Jinālaya built by Mēḍa .[5] In the Padmākshi temple inscription of Prōla II[6] of the date equal to A.D. 1117, as a subordinate to the former. In the Thousand Pillar Temple inscription[7] of Rudra appear as the main enemies of Prōla II and Rudra. It is thus to be observed th politically deprived of his original status in the rising power of the Kākatīyas.

fragmentary epigraph No. 76 of Ramagundam village, mentions certain Mahāmaı āja, who bears the titles similar to those of Mēḍarāja of Polavāsa mentioned ı-*varādhīśvara, Suvarṇa-Garuḍa-dhvaja, Śrī Satyanārāyaṇa*. In the Thous iption of Kākati Rudra, Prōla II is said to have made one Ēḍa, flee from the battle

IV. No. 1071.
ıgal Ins. No. 21
No. 26
ı Ins. (below).
ıdhrica I p. 111 ff.
ıgal Ins. No. 22,
lo. 36.

identity of this chief is not properly solved till now. The present epigraph though f s identity with certain Mahāmaṇḍalēśvara of that name ruling near Ramagundam oı erritory. Similarity in titles indicates that he might have been someway related to M It is not unlikely that all the three chiefs namely Mēḍarāja, Guṇḍarāja and Ē lding separate fiefs at Polavāsa, Manthena and Ramagundam or Peddapally respect revolted against the Chālukya king and Prōla II, as a loyal subordinate to the

THE KĀKATĪYAS

e Kākatīyas as, subordinate chiefs, have been represented by the Sanigaram epigra ve. The Karimnagar inscription of Rudra's minister Gangādhara No. 25, which is in S. 1092, furnishes detailed information regarding his family. They were the natives aki in Vēṅgidēśa. In the family of Ātrēya *gōtra* Kommanārya was born. H nd his son was Gōvinda. To Gōvinda and Turukamāmbā was born Gangādhara. Bein hara's intellectual capacities, king Prōla entrusted him with the works of the deve ḍa. His association with Rudradēva is described at length in the present inscriptio f the village Diṁḍoṁṭa as *agrahāra* to brahmaṇas and the construction of Trikūṭ a by the minister Gangādhara, on the occasion of his being appointed as Governo king with Nagarūru as capital. He is also said to have constructed a temple savа in Anumakoṇḍa and some other temples at various places. Epigraph No. 27 gmentary, seems to be of the reign of Mahadēva. The Śaka date is not clear but a when verified tallies with A.D. 1197.

e Katakūru epigraph, No. 29 of the reign of Gaṇapatidēva, furnishes a lengthy acc d Malyāla chiefs, two subordinate families under the Kākatīyas. Their gene n is given as follows :

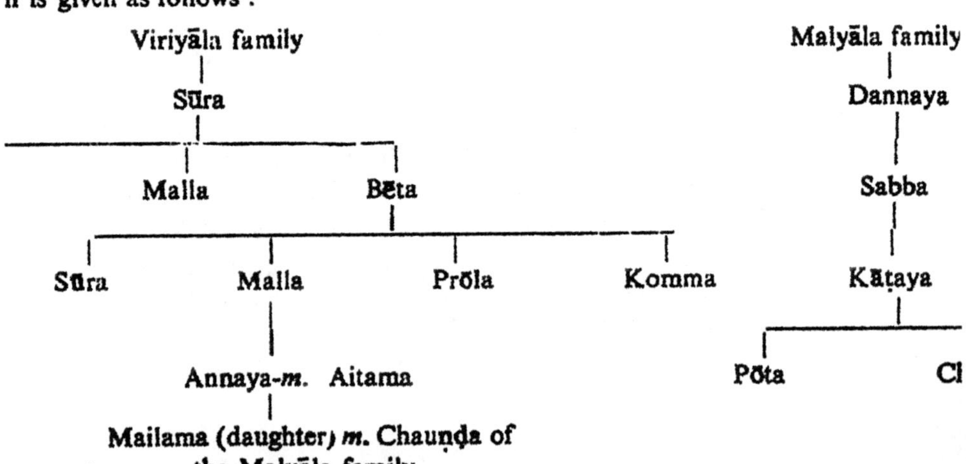

. Srinivasachari's statement that Mailama was married to Dannaya of the Mal p. 8) is due to oversight and hence to be given up. The chronology al relationship, because Mailama is said to have built temples and made certain to A.D. 1202, and 1205 which according to the Kondaparty inscription tally wi

Danna's great grandson Chaunda. The Viriyāla family in this record begins ful fight with the warring chiefs made the king Bhīma flee from the battle and event, obviously refers to the famous engagement that took place between Kākat ri Bhīmadēva Chōḍa, described at length in the former's Thousand Pillar Temple have been an elder contemporary of Kākati Rudra, whose invasion over Kand to have taken place some time before A.D. 1160. Sūra's grandson was Malla, wl as the donor in the present record. The present reference of Sūra's battle with Bhīr il in deriving a probable date of the event. This line of the members of the Vi tagged with the three members Sūra, Bēta and Malla of the Gudur inscription of Kur C.V.49 or A.D. 1124, for, Malla the last member is said to have installed the deity iru in the 49th Chālukya Vikrama year whereas his grandfather Sūra if identific n the Katakur record cannot be placed in about A.D. 1160 as said above.

ie Gōdiśāla (Upparapally) epigraph (No. 30) set up by Rājanāyaka's son Kātaya, i D. 1236, records his endowments to the god Pañchalingāla. It narrates at length t Rājanāyaka. He is said to have beheaded Godhumarātl, in the battle at Bokkera driven away certain Padirāya and made a gift of perpetual lumps to the god Bhī am.[1] Rājanāyaka was the minister of Gaṇapati's commander Rēcherla Rudra. Ga rd is stated to be the son of Rudra contrary to the well established fact that he was M ad of questioning the truthfulness of the statement, it seems reasonable to suppose t ssues might have adopted Gaṇapati as his son.

e Yelgedu epigraph (No. 37) furnishes an interesting information that (one of) Pra āja's queen was Lakumādēvi who is said to have granted remission of certain levies *ika, kaṭnam, pullari* etc., to the temple of Rāmanāthadēva for the merit of animgāru.

THE VIJAYANAGARA KINGS

e Kālēsvaram inscription (No. 45) belongs to the Vijayanagara king Dēvarāya. Sanskrit verse in *Śārdūlavikrīḍita* metre and records that king Dēvarāya son of ating the festival of *digvijaya* (conquest of the earth) at Kāleśvara, on the bank o iri) made the gift of *Tulāpurusha* on a date corresponding to Wednesday, 28th Febı *purusha* is one of the sixteen *mahādānas* (noble charities) prescribed by Hindu cano *ras*) and generally performed by royal dignitaries by giving in charity a lump of go at of the donor.

e inscription is of immense historical importance as it brings to light for the fi known expedition of Dēvarāya over Teliṅgāṇa. Dēvarāya who is stated to be is obviously Dēvarāya I. At the time of the expedition that is A.D. 1397, Harihara I npire and Dēvarāya was governing the province of Udayagiri. Kālēśvaram where t celebrated the festival of *digvijaya* was situated in the territories of the Velama kings a ole inscription of Anapōta Nāyaka dated A. D. 1369.[1] The cause of enmity be gs and the Rāyas of Vijayanagara was on account of the former's alliance with the Gulbarga, the hereditary foes of the Rāyas. This alliance was extremely disliked by I

---

es of Telingana Ins., Part III pp. 119-124.

ı advantage to the Sulṭāns in their wars with the Vijayanagara. Harihara II mad break this alliance. The expedition described in the present epigraph is one of suc last years of his reign Harihara II had a favourable opportunity caused by t in the Bahmani kingdom. During the last year of the reign of Mahammad II t Sagar, but the Sulṭan somehow managed himself to retain the fort. His two s Shams-ud-din ruled the kingdom in succession for a few months each and were a result of a revolution in the palace. It was the opportune time for Harihara II t ıe Velamas, as the latter could not get much help from their ally. To accomplish o expeditions against the Velamas simultaneously, one from south under his son or of Udayagiri and the other from west under his heir apparent, Bukka II. Of , the former culminated triumphantly at Kālēśvaram on the banks of the rive ·ibed in the record under consideration. How Dēvarāya effected the passage of e Reḍḍi territory, before he reached Teliṅgāṇa whether by peaceful agreement . scertained.

P. V. P. S

—o—

DHARMAPURI
KORATLA
POLASA
JAGTIAL
GANGADHARA
KURKYALA
VEMULAWADA
SIRSILLA
KARIM NAGAR
HAGHUR
PEDDAPALLI
MUHULAGUTTA
RAMAGUNDAM
MYDARAM
RAMAGIRI
MANTHANI
KALESWAR
PRATAPAGIR
JAMMIKUNTA
SANGARAM
GOUISALA
GODAVARI
MANER
B.W.

INSCRIPTIONS OF ANDHRA PRADESH

Karimnagar District

No. 1

(*A. R. No. 46 of 1969*)

KARIMNAGAR

On a stone lying in the local Museum.

Ṡ. 869; Parābhava, Kārtika ba. 11, Sōmavāra [**A.D. 946;** other detai
Chāḷukyas of Vēmulavāḍa
Arikesari (II)

The record begins with the mention of Juddhamalla, his son Narasiṁha, his son .
.ddega. His son was Arikēsari, who bore the titles, *Pāṁbarāṅkuśa*, *Ammanagandhı*
ıa, *Guṇārṇava*, and *Tribhuvanamalla*. He is said to have made a gift of fifty *mattı*
lage Aripanapaḷḷi to a brahman named Dhārapayya son of Appaṇayya and grar
ı of Kauśika *gōtra* and a resident of Nūtulapāḍu. The five introductory verses ε
ı's *Vikramārjunavijaya* (I-15, 31, 41, 42 and 50).

TEXT

SIDE

1. స్వస్తి శ్రీ మచ్చళు
2. క్య వంస[వార్ధి]మూ
3. మృతకిరణ నెనిప శా
4. న్తి యనొళ కొణ్డి మహియొ
5. ళాత్మవంశ సిఖామణి[జ]
6. సమెసెయొ జుద్ధమల్లనెగ
7. ఢ్డిం*[1]* ఆత్మ భవ నాధరాధి
8. ప నాత్మజ నజనవాహుపృథుళ
9. గీరతనళ రామాత్మజ[రనిళ]
10. సి నెగడ్డి మహాత్మ నరసి[ఙ్గ]
11. నళివి[నొళ్ప]రమాత్మం[2]*

12. ఆజాకయ్యొగ మావసుధా
13. జయా వల్లభంగ మతివిళ
14. ది(ద)యళో రాజితనెని పరికే
15. సరి రాజ త్తేజోగ్నిమా(మ)గ్నరి
16. పున్నృప[ళ]లభం+[3]*మగ నా[ళె]
17. నాగి వాగళెనెగత్తెయొ ళ్బర
18. దెసక దొళ్నెగళె మగంస మ
19. నెనె పుట్టలొడం కోళ్మగగొణ్డు
20. దు భువనభవన మరికేసరి
21. యా॥[4]* చాగద కంభ

SECOND SIDE

22. చాగద కంభ[1] మ[న్ని ఱిసిఱి]
23. రద ళాసన మన్నెగట్బికో
24. ళ్ళొగద మణ్డలం గళనె[కొ]
25. ణ్డు జగత్రితయంగళొళ్ జ
26. ళక్కా గ[ర]*నూద బద్దెగ ని నా న
27. రసింఘుని నత్తనాల్వ రిం మే
28. గెపొదళ్డచాగ దొళమొన్ది
29. దఱిరదొళంగుణార్ణ్ణవం[5]*
30. స్వస్తి సమధిగత పఞ్చమ
31. హాళబ్ద మహాసమన్తాధి
32. పతి సమస్త భువన సంస్తూ
33. య మాన చాళుక్య వంశోద్భ
34. వం పొంబరాంకుళ నమ్మన గ
35. న్ధవారణం గన్ధేభవిద్యాధ
36. ర నుదా త్త నారాయణం ప్రత్య
37. క్ష[వార్ధమె]యా రూఢ సర్వ్వ
38. జ్ఞ గుణనిధి గుణార్ణ్ణవ ప్రి
39. యగళ్లం త్రిభువన మల్లం

1. Redundant

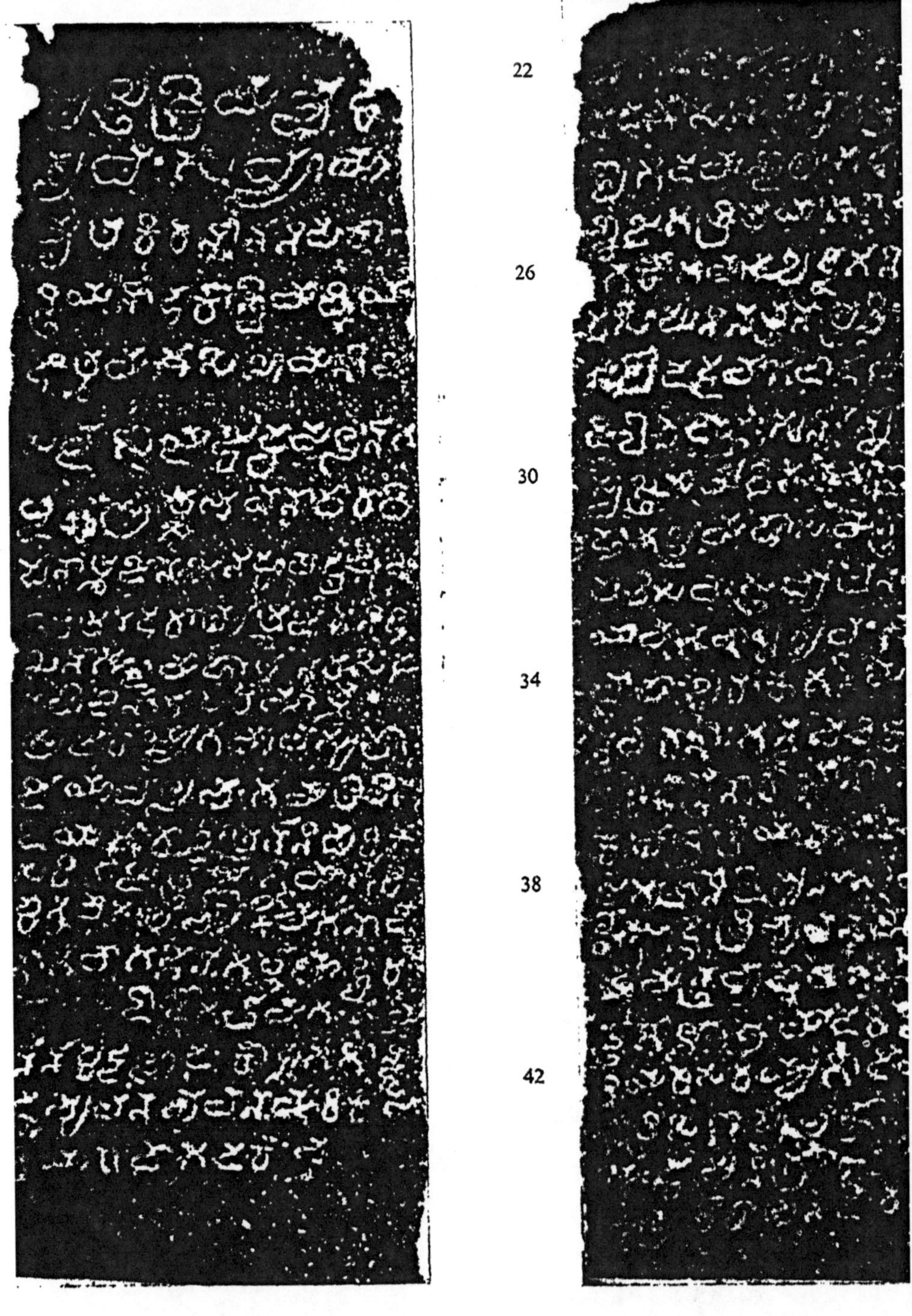

Ins. 1. Karimnagar Inscription of Arikēsarin II.

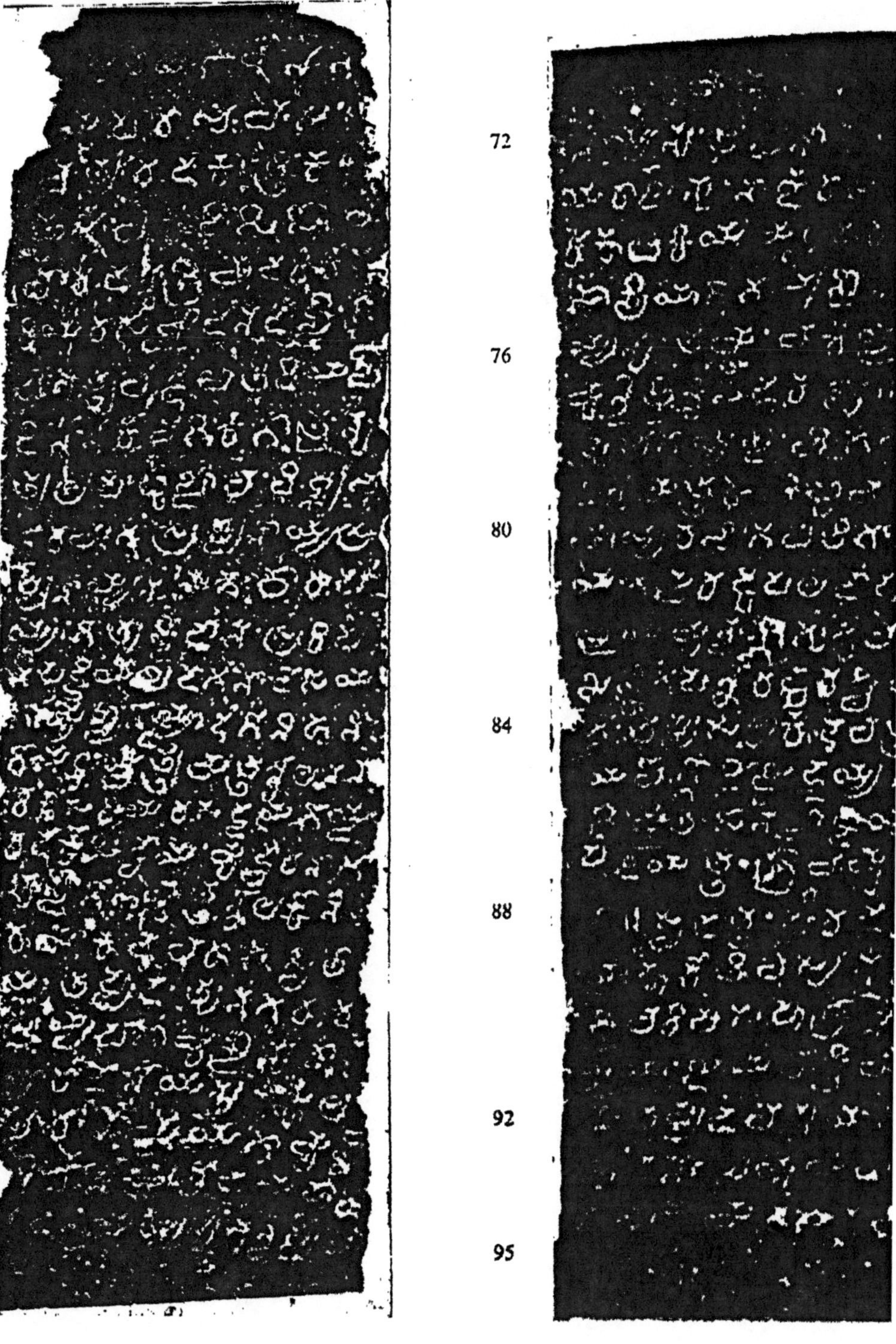

III SIDE IV SIDE

Ins. 1. Karimnagar Inscription of Arikēsarin II.

40. సామన్త చూడామణినో[డి]
41. త్తె గెల్వం శ్రీమదరికేస
42. రియరసరఁయ్యంగొడెయ
43. నెత్తి సి [ఇప్పఱ త్తిచ్ఛా - -]
44. ఘుం దుష్ట నిగ్రహా వి [-]
45. ష్ట ప్రతిపాలన దిం[రా]జ్య
 - - -

THIRD SIDE

46. [స]క వషఱ[ల]ఱ నె
47. య పరాభవ సం
48. వత్సరద కాత్త్రిఱక బ
49. వహుళ ఏ[కా ద]సి సోమ
50. వారదన్దు శ్రీమదరికేస
51. రియరస[చ్చాఱ]దన దణ్డి[గొ]
52. [విణ]త్తు వ[ళ్ళే]అ తటియబీ
53. [డినొళ్]కౌశిక గోత్ర నూ
54. తులపాటిఱ బోవం వి[ష్ణు]భ
55. ట్టరమగం అ[ప్ప]ణయ్య అ
56. ప్పణయ్యన మగం ధారప
57. య్యంగెతు[ష్టి]దానం అరిప
58. [న]పళ్లియ బడగణ దెసెయ
59. [గాముణనెయ్దు] ళంగెనిళనా
60. రెయె లఱ్వ్వుత్తుమత్తన్నెఱలనన
61. రికేసరియరస ర్దఱ యొంగె ర్దయ
62. రుదక్కెసిద్ధాయంముద్దరణగా
63. ముణ్డగె ఇమ్మత్తన్నెఱలక్కెనీ
64. [రు పంకుళ]వరు ఈ స్థితి
65. యంతప్పద తు నగరూర

66. అయ్యపగాముణ్డను శా[పు]
67. [లూ]ర దెన్నెయను మూాల
68. [గూ]రపోమయగాముణ్డె
69. [-----]ద మహా[జ]
70. న దిణ్డమయ్యను కన్దప్పఁ య

FOURTH SIDE

71. [తాఱూ] రమహాజంకస
72. [న]య్యనుం అప్పణను చణ్డి
73. యరాజనుం నాజ రాజను
74. [రే]కుఱికియ మల్లపరాజను
75. సాఱియాగె గాముణ్డనె చ[ట్ట]
76. య్యనుం తమ్మంమకయ్య
77. మునిల్ది క్కిసిదకమ్మ॥ చను
78. [లూ]ర గాముణ్డంచింగపులిగె
79. [ఒను] మత్తరు విఱు మడియు
80. మాయ్యరభోగ పతి గాముణ్డ
81. య[గమె]ర డుపలదొళంకె
82. ఱెయ మున్ద[ణ్ణె]గుడువనేల్లు
83. ఖణ్డుగ పన్నెరడు[ఈ]స్థితియా
84. గ్గె తప్ప సల్ల కుళ వత్త ళె
85. య పెగ్గెఁ డెజుట్టయ్యన సం
86. ధిష్టిత సేనబొజయ నా
87. పదియత్తం శ్రీమమ్నబరె
88. దొ॥ స్వదత్తంపరదత్తంవ
89. యోహరేతి వసున్దరి ష
90. ష్టివరిష సహస్రాణి వి
91. ష్టయాం జాయతే క్రిమి॥ ఇ

దంతప్పద వ ప్రయాగెయు

బారణాసియు మడిదపా

ప మ క మ ర స ర జె య

మికెక్కి ॥

No. 2

(*A. R. No. 170 of 1966*)

VEMULAVADA

On a stone pillar set up in the Rājēśvara temple.

ıdated ·
ıāḷukyas of Vēmulavāḍa
ikēsari (II)

e record gives the genealogy of this branch of Chāḷukyas beginning from Vinay
la who is said to have ruled the country of *Sapādalaksha* and made his elephants
with oil in the town Pōdana. He also seized the fort of Chitrakūṭa after defeati
on was Arikēsarin who by his prowess captured the entire Vēṅgi country. His son
Rājāditya who was followed by (his son) Yuddhamalla. Baddega and again Yudd
ndson succeeded him in order. Next, followed Narasiṁhadēva who defeated the
and collected tributes from them. He also defeated the army of the Gūrjara king wh
n and set up a pillar of victory on the Kāḷapriya mount. His son was Arikēsarin
he *sāmantas* and *daṇḍamukhyas* (generals) killed Pannyārya along with his fol
from the wrath of Gōvindarāja. He married Rēvakanirmaḍi, the daughter of
titles stated in the record are *Pāṁbarāṅkuśa*, *ammanagandhavāraṇa*, *gandhēbha-*
ajña, *guṇanidhi*, *guṇārṇava* and *Tribhuvanamalla*. At the request of his *tantrapāla*
gamārya, the king made a gift of hundred *nivartanas* of *bhū-kshētra* and eight *ni*
ētra in the north-east direction of Lēmbuḷavāṭa for maintaining a choultry for
The *sthānapatis* of the four temples of Rājēśvara, Āditya, Baddegēśvara and N
ascetics named Mallikārjuna *vyaktaliṅgi*, Vidyārāśi *vyākhyāni bhaṭṭāraka* and
e stated as witnesses.

e *siddhāya* of the said land is fixed as twelve *drammas*.

TEXT

శ్రీమాన్వానుస్తమోహాంశా దైత్యదప్పజ హారత్ప్రి [రః]

లోకైకలోచన ఛాయా దపాయా ద్భువనత్రయం [॥]

స్వస్తి సమస్త విబుధ జనసంస్తూయమాన స్వక

4. ళ కళా కమలై కరాజహంసః కంసమథనైవ (నఇవ)
5. కమళాకరీకృత వక్షస్థళ స్థాణు రివ భా (భ) స్మ
6. సాత్కృత సమస్తారి పుర ప్రచణ్డ శ్చ వృద్ధోదయ ప్రబోధితా
7. శేష ప్రవాహో[1] ంభోజాన్వర్థీ కృత వినయాదిత్య
8. నామధేయ శ్చసాధితాశేషదిగ్మణ్డలశ్చ ప[ర]
9. మణ్డలైకరామ శ్చాళుక్య కుళతిళకః శ్రీయుద్ధ
10. మల్లో నామ రాజా బభూవ॥ సోఽయం కిళో (లా) ళాస ద
11. నన్యళాస్యాం సపాదలక్షాం క్షితి మక్షతాజ్ఞః స
12. మస్తరాజేన్ద్రకిరీటకోటి మాణిక్యరా (ర) శ్మి శ్చ (ప్ర) స
13. ర (రా)చ్చిర్త తాంఘ్రిః॥ యత్పోదనే సౌధమయీ గజానాం వి
14. ధాయ వాపీ మపి తైలపూరై స్సన్సర్వసేకం స
15. తతం వితేనే చాన్ద్రసైః కుచానా మరిసున్దరీణాం॥
16. స చిత్రకూటం బహు చిత్రకూటం శక్య[ం]సురేన్ద్రై రపి
17. నోపయాతుం త్రివర్గయుక్త శ్చణతారివర్గ
18. స్స్వభావదుర్గం కిళ తం జహార॥ తస్యాత్మజో ద
19. క్షిణ బాహు దణ్డ చణ్డాసిధారాహత వైరి
20. ష[ణ్డో] [బళా] ద్గృహీతాఖిళ వేఙ్గిదేశ శ్చా
21. తి స్మ పృథ్వీ మరికేసరీశః [॥]* భూయో స్మాన్న
22. రసింహవర్మ్మా నృపతిర్భూమిం సమాపాదయ
23. న్నాజాదిత్య ఇతి క్షమాపతి రతా(తః) శ్రీయుద్ధమ
24. ల్లో నృపః[।] త్యక్త్వా యేన దధీచి [క] ర్ణ శిబ[య]* స్త్యాగైః
25. భూభుజ శ్చాళ్చా ద్బద్దేగ [కల్పదారు రవరః] శ్రీయుద్ధ
26. మల్ల [శ్చ]నః॥ [త]త స్సరాజన్య శిరోమణీనాం పాదార
27. విన్దేన రుచో హార ద్యః బభూవ నామ్నా సరసింహదేవః స్తం
28. భా త్యుపమా శ్లోక భృతా[వివాద్య]॥ యః[స్స]స్త దుస్సాధ్య తర

1. Dr. N. Venkataramanayya suggests ప్రవాహాంభోజా–*The Chalukyas*

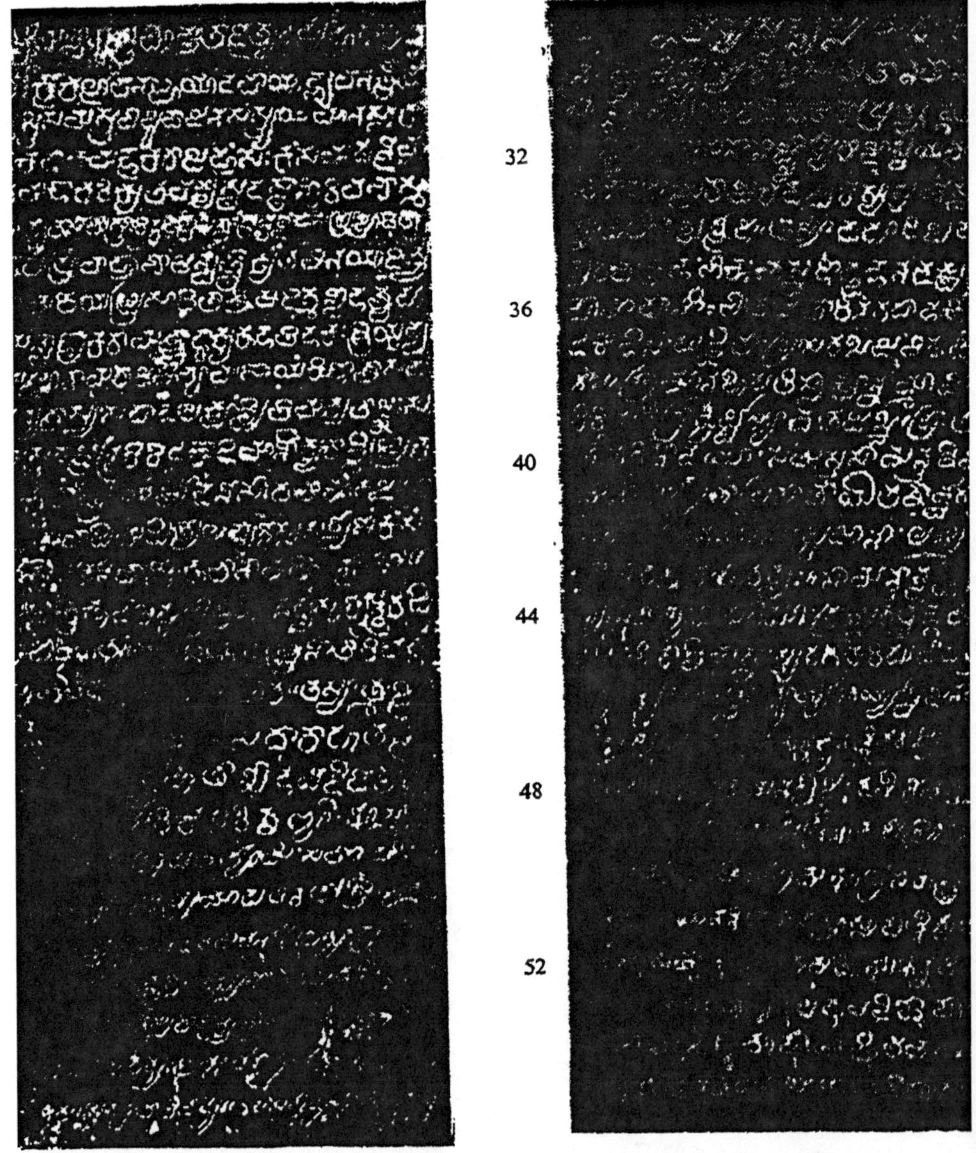

I SIDE

II SIDE

Ins. 2. Vemulavada Inscription of Arikēsarin II.

SECOND SIDE

29. ప్రాణాన్నిర్జిత్య సద్య స్సమరాంగ
30. ణేషు విన్యస్య కే హస్త మతోనతానాం
31. స్తానాన్మాళవ(వా)న్యః కరదీచకార॥ ప్రత్యుద్గతాం
32. గూర్జర రాజసేనాం నిర్జిత్య రాజా స్వయ మ(మే)క
33. ఏవ కాళప్రియే రాజకదంబకస్య స్తంభే స్వ[శౌ]
34. ర్య్య[ర్గ]విలిలేఖ శైశే॥ తస్యోదపాది బళవ
35. త్పరచక్రకుంభి కుంభస్థళోద్దళన దక్షక్ర
36. పాణపాణిః క్షితానతారినరపాళకిరీ
37. ట కోటి సంఘట్టితాంఘ్రి సరసీజవిరాజమా
38. నః॥ శ్రీమాన్మహీపతి స్సాంతహూ న్నామ్మా(మ్నా) వీ[రో]
39. రివేసరీ ప్రాదుర్బభూవ తేజస్వీ ప్రాతా(త)
40. ర్భానురివోదయాం(యాత్॥) సమస్త సామన్త శిఖా
41. మణీనాం ప్రభాప్రపాతాయిత శార్వరాస్త్రం(రాం సః)
42. సదారినారీ నయనాంబుజానాం లక్ష్మింహి
43. మాసార ఇవా హారద్యః॥ సామన్తా న్దడ్డము
44. ఖ్యా న్నిజభుజపరిఘాం ప్రస్ఫురత్ఖడ్గ ధారా
45. ం నీరాంభోరాశి మగ్నాం స్తురగ కరి ఘటాపత్తి స
46. ంప త్తియుక్తాన్ కృత్వా పన్నాయ్యయ్యర్ మాయ్యర్ం స్వజన పరి
47. జనై స్సన్నిహ త్యాజితంగే॥ కృద్ధే గోవిన్దరాజే శరణ
48. ముపగతో రక్షితో యేన బిజ్జః[॥]దేవీం రేవకనిమ్మ
49. డిం క్షితి పతే రిద్దనస్య పుత్రీమ్నుతాం పౌలోమీ మివ
50. వాసవ[ః]శ్రియ మివ శ్రీమన్మరధ్వంసకః స్త్రీరత్నం
51. పరిణీయ[యే]న నితరం తస్యా స్సపత్నీకృతా[నా]
52. నం సప్తసముద్రముద్రిత మహీ మ్మానోన్నతే నాధు
53. నా॥ తేన క్షితానతాఖిళబళవదిళాపాళ మౌ
54. ళి మాణిక్యరశ్మిమాలాలాళిత చరణకమ

THIRD SIDE

56. రక్షణదక్షకౌక్షేయకోపల తీక్ష్యణదక్షిణ
57. భుజాగ్రగ్రశేన కా[న్త్యా]కాన్తకాన్తాజన మనోనయ
58. న వల్లభేన కరేణుపుత్రేణేవ స్ప(స) కళ గజచి
59. కిత్సా కోవదోన(కోవిదేన)గౌతమేనేవైకశీతి రసా వ
60. ధ(ధి)విధి కుశళేన రాజాత్మజేనేవ పరీక్షా
61. విధానదక్షిణ[ః]* వార్ధశినేవ బన్ధురకమ్మార్గ
62. స్కన్దసంపన్వ(న్న)పరాయణేన ఈశ్వరేణేవ
63. విజిత మనోజేనోమాప్రియేణ చ
64. నారాయణే నేవ గోవర్ద్ధ(నే)[1]న ధరేణ చ
65. చతురాననేన(నే)వ(ం)చతురాననేనవ। సక
66. ళ కళానిళయో నవకళాధిర వ[క్త్ర]
67. ముదానన్దకరేణ కాన్తిమతా చ వనజా(జ)
68. బన్ధునేవ ప్రబోధిత బన్ధురబన్ధు వ
69. దన వనజేన నిరస్తార(రా)తి తిమిరేణ
70. చ సహస్ర కిరణవ దతుళతేజసా
71. శ్రీమదరికేసరి మహా రాజేన ।।।
72. స్వస్తిసమధి గతపంచమహాశబ్ద మహా
73. సామన్తాధిపతి సమస్త భువన సంస్తూయ[మా]
74. న చాళుక్య వంశోద్భవం పాంబరాంకుశ నమ్మన గ
75. న్ధవారణం గన్దేభ విద్యాధరనారూఢ సర్వజ్ఞ
76. నుదాత్తనారాంణం నోళుత్తె గెల్వాం గుణనిధి గుణా
77. ర్ణవం శర[ణా*]గత వజ్ర పంజరం ప్రియగళ్లం
78. త్రిభువన మల్ల సామన్తచూడామణి శ్రీ
79. మదరికేసరియరసర తత్పాద పద్మోప
80. జీవిసమస్త రాజ్యభరనిరూపిత మహా
81. సన్ధివిగ్రహా పదవీ ప్రతిష్ఠితం సమస్త

1. (నే) superfluous

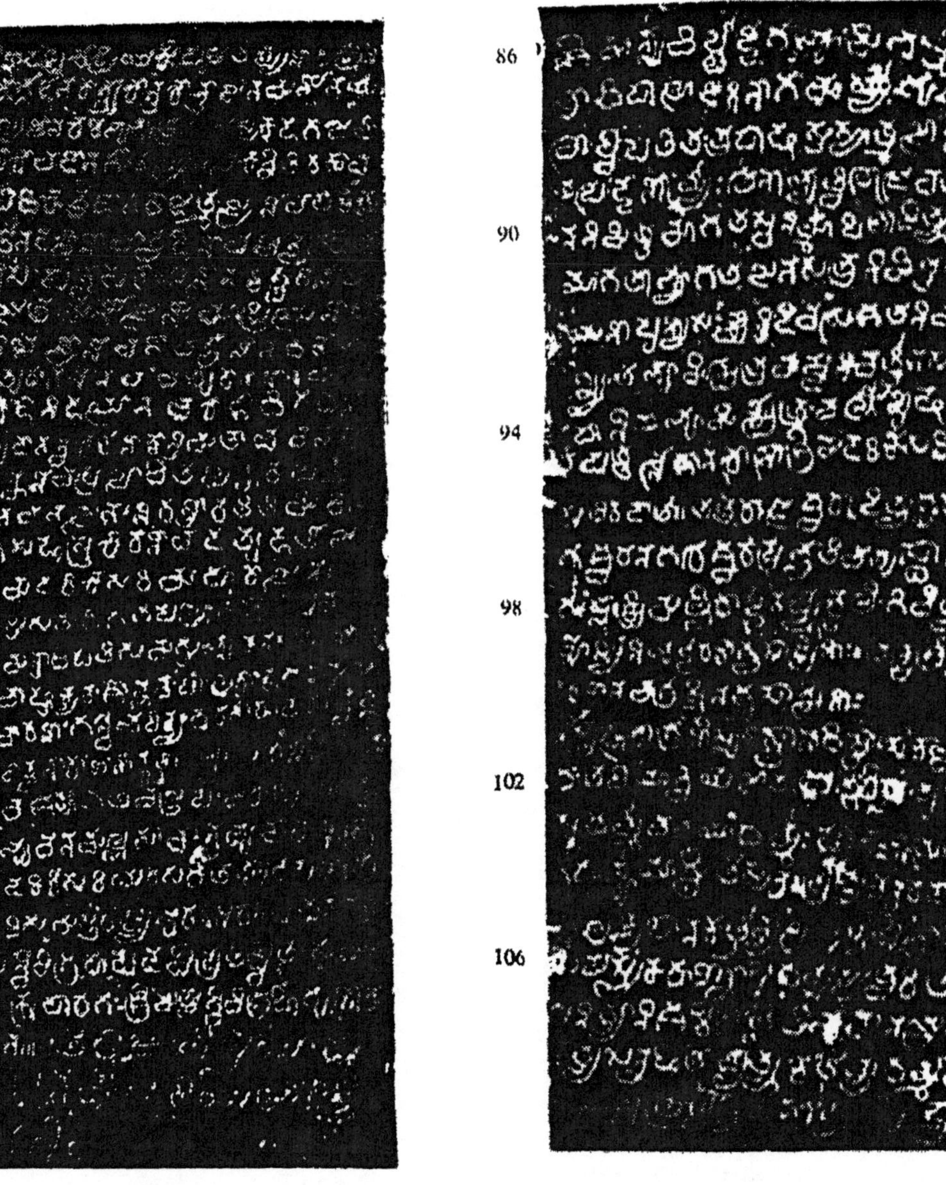

III SIDE   IV SIDE

Ins. 2. Vemulavada Inscription of Arikēsarin II.

82. శాస్త్రపారగం శ్రీమత్సన్ది విగ్రహిగుణాంకు
83. శేన ।।। త[తాఅంభోల్లాయవ]
84. [న్నజన పీసదియం ఆదిత్యం]
85. ˉగ బిట్ట

FOURTH SIDE

86. శ్రీమాన్సుధీ బ్బర్ద్దెగభూమి భర్త్తుస్తం
87. త్రాధిపాలో జని నాగమార్య్యః గుణార్ణ్ణ
88. వోర్వ్వీపతి తంత్రపాళ స్తస్యాత్మజో జాయ
89. తపెద్దణార్య్యః[॥] తే నాభ్యర్త్థితో దేవతా వన్ద
90. ననిమిత్త మాగత స్వనిర్మ్మాణ పితాదిత్యగృహో
91. యాగతాభ్యాగతజన సత్ర నిమిత్త ముత్తరా
92. యణపుణ్య సంక్రాన్తి దివసే శతనివర్త్తన సం
93. ఖ్యాతభూమిక్షేత్ర మష్ట నివర్త్తన సంఖ్యాత
94. పానీయ భూమిక్షేత్రం చ లేంబుళవాట
95. కవత్తనేళాన కోణే శ్రీమదరికేసరిక్షితి
96. పతి రదాత్ ॥ తత్ర రాజేశ్వరాదిత్య గృహ బద్దె
97. ˉగేశ్వర నగరేశ్వర ప్రభృతి చతుస్థానాది(ధి)వా
98. సస్సాక్షీ మల్లికార్జ్జున వ్యక్తలింగి విద్యారాశి
99. వ్యా[ఖ్యా]ని భట్టారకశ్చ సాక్షిణః॥ చన్ద్రశ్రేష్ఠిప్రభృ
100. తయోనవశ్రేష్ఠిన శ్చసాక్షిణః
101. ని[ప్పల]హైకాగ్రణీ సూ్సరి స్థానాధిష్ఠాయక(ః)స్వయం
102. తాతవీయాన్వయేజాతః పణ్డిత మునీశ్వరః
103. స్వధర్మ్మవ దయంధర్మ్మః పాళనీయోనరాధిపై[ః]*
104. నధర్మ్మార్త్థయాస్థితే స్సన్తః ప్రచ్యవన్తి కదాచన[।]
105. కాలక్షేపో న కర్త్తవ్యం ఆయుక్షీణో దినే దినే [॥]*
106. [య]మస్య కరుణ(ణా)న్నా(నా)స్తిధర్మ్మస్య త్వరితాగతం(తిః)॥[ ]
107. అనిత్యాని శరిరాణి విభవోనయ్య శాశ్వత(తః)[।]

. నిత్యంసన్నహితోమృత్యు[ః]* కర్త్తవ్య(వ్యో) ధమ్మ౯సంగ్రహ [।]*

. తస్యక్షేత్రస్య ద్వాదశ ద్రమ్మ స్సిద్ధాయః[॥]*

No. 3

(A. R. No. 178 of 1966)

KURKYALA

(Karimnagar Taluk)

On a hillock called Bommalaguṭṭa.

lated

ḷukyas of Vēmulavāḍa

:ēsari (II)

cords the installation of the images of the first and last Jaina Tīrthaṅkaras and the c called *Tribhuvanatilaka*, a tank called *Kavitāguṇārṇava* and a garden named *Mada* a son of Bhīmapayya and Abbaṇabbe and the younger brother of Pampa *alias* Kavit e inscription furnishes valuable information regarding the genealogy and the origin of aḍa poet and the author of *Vikramārjunavijaya* and *Ādipurāṇa*, whose ancestors a ged to Kamme-brāhmaṇa caste and hailed from Vaṁgipaṟṟa village in Beṁgi *nāḍu*.

Text

ఓం నమః సిద్ధేభ్యః [।]*స్వస్తి సమస్తసకళ కళా కళాపప్రవీణం భవ్యరత్నాకర[ం] గ
బెంగినాడ సప్తగ్రామగళొళగణ వంగిపఱ్ఱు కమ్మెబ్రాహ్మణం జమదగ్ని వ
శ్రీవత్సగోత్రం గుణ్డికఱ్ఱు నిడుంగొణ్డె యభిమానచన్ద్రన మమ్మం
బెళ్వొలదణ్ణిగెఱెయ జోయిస సింఘన మమ్మ౯

ళబ్బణబ్బెయమగం కౌణ్డకుణ్డెయ దేసిగగణద పొత్తగెయ బళియ పణ్డరంగ వ
ణన్ది సిద్ధాన్త భటారర గుడ్డం జినవల్లభం సబ్బినాడ నట్టనడువణ ధమ్మపురద దు
వృషభగిరి యెంబనాది సంసిద్ధ తీర్థద దక్షిణ దిశాభాగ దీపిద్ధ శిలెయొళ్ తమ్మ కులదైవ
జినబింబంగళుమం చక్రేశ్వరియుమం పెఱవుం జినప్రతి

మెగళుమం త్రిభువన తిలక మెంబ బసదియుమం కవితాగుణార్ణవ మెంబ కెఱెయు
విళాస మెంబబనముమం మాడిసిదం। వృత్తం॥ భ్రాత ర్ధమ్మపురం ప్రయా
జైనాభిషేకోత్సవ క్షీరప్లావితతుంగశృంగ వృషభక్షోణీద్ధ మీక్షామహే యాత్రాయ
భవ్యజనతా సన్మాన దానోద్యతం పంపాయ్యా౯

నుజ మత్ర భీమతనుజం పశ్యాత్మ రత్నాకరం॥ [౧]*గీతం గాతు మనేక భేదసుభగం
సోచ్చావచం వాచా వాచయితుం ప్రియాణి వదితుం సాధూపతత్తు౯ం సతాం భో

మంగనా రమయితుం పూజాంవిధాతుం జినే జానీతే జినవల్లభ బ్బిరమిదం పం:
నుజః॥౨॥ అజస్ర జినవన్దనాగత మునీ

శ్వరశ్రావక ప్రజాస్తవరవ ప్రతిధ్వనిత శబ్ద కోళాహలై [ః*]అధిష్ఠిత దిగంబరో వృషభ
స్స్వయం పరాం వదతి వాచకాభరణకీర్త్తిః మాకళ్పతః॥[౩*॥]బగెయ లళుంబవి
నాబ్బఁగె వొబ్బఁగెగాసెయల్తు దిట్టగె పొలనల్తు నీళ్దసఱియో ళ్జినబింబమ నీతనిగ
దప్పొనెన్దుబగెవన్నెవరం జినబింబ

మల్లితొట్టగె నెగట్ధిబింబివేం చరిత మచ్చరియోజినవల్లభేన్ద్రినం॥ [॥*౪]ఇదు కవితా
వన కీర్త్తి [౯]యమూర్త్తి [౯*]వొలాగి దక్షిణార్ద్ధఁద వృషభాద్రియక్కె వృష
సనాథమెంబలంపొడవె నిజద్విజావసథ పర్వ్వఁతమం జినచైత్యమాగె మాడిద జి
జినవల్లభనప్పుదు మొన్దుభోద్యమో॥ [౫*] చదురమయ్మెయ సత్క

విత్వద సన్ద పంపనతమ్మ నోర్వ్వఁదె పొగత్తెయె బాజిసల్బరెయ ల్కవిత్వదతత్వది
నేర్వ్వఁడెపేటిలుర్వ్విఁగ పూర్వ్వఁమాగిరె బల్లొనప్పుదటి నొర్వ్వఁనె వాగ్వధూ
జినవల్లభం॥ [౬॥]* వినుత చళుక్యవంశపతి మిక్కరికేసరి సన్ద విక్రమార్జున
ధమ్మఁపురం మెన్దు మదేయ మిదెన్దు కీర్త్తిఁశాసన మెనెకొట్ట శాసనద పంప

న నంబిదుదొన్దు జైనశాసనద నెగత్తెయం వృషభపర్వ్వఁతమన్తదుతానె పేటిదే॥
గెల్గాళిపుగల్పతంగ కిరణం సారల్మిగం పాఱలా గసదొ శ్ళృక్కిగళల్లి సల్లవెనిసిటి
ధమ్మఁ దొళ్జసమం పొంపుటి మాడెమెచ్చి హారిగం పంపంగె గొట్టా ద్విజావసథ
న్నెగత్తెయ కళాపగ్రామమం పొల్తుదో॥ [౮] బరదుదె

తాంబ్రశాసన మదేయమె ధమ్మఁవురంనెగత్తెవె త్తరిగన కొట్టుదే నెగట్ధి పంపన
మెన్దు నిమ్మరుళె పలమ్మెఁయుం పలబరం బెన గొళ్ళదె పోగినోడ సున్దర వృషభ
శిళాతళదొళ్బరె దక్కరంగళం॥ [౯*] కన్దం॥ జినభవనంబు లెత్తించుట జినపూజల్సే
జినమునులకు నర్త్తిన యన్నదానం బీవుట జినవల్లభు బోలంగలరె

జినధర్మ్మఁ పరుల్॥ [౧౦]* దినకరుసరి వెల్గుదుమని జినవల్లభునొట్టనెత్తు జితకవిన
జుల్గలరే ధాత్రిం వినితిచ్చిదు ననియవృత్త విబుధ కవీన్ద్రుల్॥ [౧౧॥] ఒకొక్కకొ

No. 4

(A. R. No. 169 of 1966)

VEMULAVADA

On a pedestal of a Jaina image kept in the Rājēśvara temple.

Chāḷukyas of Vēmulavāḍa

Baddega

The inscription records the construction of Śubhadhāma Jinālaya by the king
:ya lineage and the lord of *Sapāda laksha* 'one and a quarter lakh' region for the favou
ēva, the head of Gauḍa-*sangha*. Yuddhamalla's name is also indistinctly seen. The d
e author of *Yaśastilaka champu*, a Sanskrit work of the medieval period.

TEXT

1. సపాద లక్షవ్యావత్తిః [- - - యుద్ధమల్లతః]
2. బద్దెగా [జో్క] భవద్భూపశ్చాళుక్య కుళ భాస్కరః [।]
3. గౌడసంఘాధిప శ్రీమత్సోమదేవాయ సూరయే
4. తే నాయం భూభుజాకారి శుభధామ జినాళయః [॥]

No. 5

(A. R. No. 192 of 1965)

REPAKA

On a pillar lying in the field near the Middle School.

S. 888; Prabhava, Phālguṇa śu. 13, Bṛihaspativāra (Thursday) [A. D. 968 Feb. 14,
Chāḷukyas of Vēmulavāḍa
Arikēsari (III)

Damaged. Introduces a [chief] named Śrimat Vujaya who bears a string of title
of lands to a Jinālaya built by him. The latter half refers to the genealogy of
s of the Jaina faith who were holding a fief comprising Atukūru-70 and Pammi-
nbers of the family are Kāma, Rāma, Tukkaya Revaṇa, Puṇyarāma, Kommayya
y certain line of Jaina ascetics is also given. In the end it is said that the temple
; Arikēsari.

IDE

TEXT

1. స్వస్తి సకనృప కాలా [క్రా]
2. న్త సంవత్సర శతంగళు
3. [౮౮] ౮ నెయ ప్ర[భ]వ సం[వ]

]ంద ఫాల్గుణ [శు]ద్ధ త్రయో
ము [బృ] [హ*] స్పతి వారం స్వస్తి
ేక గుణగణాళంక్రి[త]
్యత కీర్త్తి యశేష [క]
;]ణాభ్యుదయ [సంపన్నస్వా]
)] భృత్యం పతిహిత చిత్ర[ం]
[న ?] ణ్డం [నడెదన్తి గణ్డం]
జనప్రియం బన్ధు కల్పద్రు
[కా వ] రా భరణం సమ్య[క్త]
]షణం శ[వు] చ[గంగా సుత -]
పతు పార్థ్థం[బట్ట] చి
ంణి సౌభాగ్య గు[డ్డి] గ[ం]
మత్ వుజయగ[ణ్డ]
;రోత్తరం పె [ట్టి] నాగ్గిం [ము]
ణ్డి పట్ట కట్టిన[- ఖ] శివుత్తు
నాలయ మనెత్తిసి
గెకొట్ట పన్నెసెపన్ని
ఖగన నీన్నేల కరి
నేల సలువత్తుమ
ం బెళ్వాటి - వ
మత్తురు [ఇ]
త్తు - -] ల్మమనె
[న్వె] సనం గాణువ [లి] ఎ
బసది [గె] ల్లె [ల్ల]
స ఇఖణ్డుగ దం
నిన్నేలం ఇప్పత్తుమ
ం బెల్వాలంవెల్లాల ప

SECOND SIDE

1. [ట్టు] పన్నె సె [యంనీర్న్నేలని]
2. ఖణ్డుగు [- ప్ప] త్తు
3. మత్తరు బెల్వాలం [మణాం]
4. [సపు - పన్న సెయుం] నీర్న్నేల
5. నిఖణ్డుగ ఇప్పత్తు మ
6. త్తరు [బెన్వాల - -]
7. పన్న సెయ నీర్న్నేలని [-]
8. బెల్వాల నిప్పత్తు [మత్త -]
9. ఇన్తి భూమియ [ం - -]
10. - మగప - - -
11. [-] శెయుం - -
12. యిస్తితి గెతప్పిద రు - -
13. రణాసియు ప్రయాగయు
14. [......పమ హాః......]
15. సామాన్యోయం ధర్మ్మసేతు న్నృపా
16. ణాం కాలేకాలేపాలనీయో [భ]
17. వద్భి [స్సర్వ్వా] నేతాన్భావినః పా
18. ర్థ్థివేంద్రా న్భూయోభూయో
19. యాచతే రామభద్ర। బహుభిర్వ్వసు
20. [-] దత్తా రాజభి స్సగరాదిభి
21. యస్యయస్య యదాభూమి
22. స్తస్య తస్య తదాఫలం। స్వదత్తం
23. పరదత్తం వాయో హరేతి వసు
24. న్ధరాం షష్టిర్వ్వర్ష సహస్రాణి
25. విష్టాయాం జాయతే కృమిః॥
26. మద్వంశజాః పరమహీప
27. తివంశజావా పాపాదపేత మ

నసోఖువి ఖావిభూపాః యేపాల [య]
న్తి మమధమ్మ౯ మిదం సమస్తం
తేషాం మయా విరచితోంజలిరే
షమూర్ధ్ని౯॥ సాయణయ్యా
...............కణ్డ
బరిసిదకం [బ]॥......దిగె
గళు.........గళు రాజ
వను.........మ్మ౯ ర......
ఒను విన్నన్త బల - నుం
...............మంగళ.........

›E

శ్రీమద్విట్ట కులాం
బరుభానూ [-] ల్వాతు
కూర సప్తతి పమ్మిద్వా
దళకయుగ్మ దేశగ్రా
మాధిపో జినేన్ద్ర ధ [మ్మ౯]
నుగ [-]॥ చతుర్వి౯ధ
శ్రావకధ [మ్మ౯] సంపదో
మహోధ్వజోత్తపన ల
బ్ధ వణ్న౯ [కొ]గుణాష్టకా
లంకృత దృష్టి పుణ్యారా
మప్రియె త్రాత్రిక ధ
వ్యరామో॥ తత్పుత్రతూ
క్కయనామ తూక్కయా
గ్రజ రేవణం తేనాగ్ర
జన్మ తుక్కయ్యాం తత్పు
త్రపుణ్యారామయోః॥

17. పుణ్యారామ ప్రియో పు
18. త్రో రేవణయ్య మహాబలీ
19. సజ్జనాభరణం నామ
20. శ్రావకృద్ధర్మ్మ వత్సలైః
21. తేనాగ్రజశ్చ గొమ్మయ్య
22. శ్రీ [ముదే] పుణ్య రామవత్
23. ధన్యారామోచ చత్వారః
24. చర్వ ద్విసమోనుత [ః]॥

FOURTH SIDE

Illegible

1. - - - న్న త - మము
2. - - - - -
3. - - - - -
4. ణ - - - - - ॥
5. - - - - - ప్ర
6. యులు - - శై - పా
7. కముజతో- - - -
8. - బ్రణి - త - -
9. వరాజసుతః - -
10. శివక్షేచ పార్థివా
11. [వన స] మ్యక్తసుద్ధ -
12. కారిత జైన మన్దిరం॥
13. తస్యాన్తి [సన] గణ- - -
14. పటికా - - -
15. - - బసిదెణ
16. తచ్ఛిష్య రామభద్రజా
17. తే నశిష్యస్య విజ్ఞేయ
18. శా - - - మహామునిః॥

తత్శిష్య వయ్యఁ భద్రాఖ్యా
[- - - -] సమోపమో
[జి] నసేనాయ్యఁ ఛాత్రేణ
రచితం సా[య]ణమ్మ [హా]
రెసి॥ మునిషు
ప్రభవామొ [-] కొట్టిమొ
శ్రీ అరికేసరి రాజ్యేనా
నరనాజ్యేన మన్ది [- -]

No. 6

(*A. R. No. 171 of 1966*)

VEMULAVADA

(*Sircilla Taluk*)

On a broken stone in the tank

Date missing

Western Chāḷukya

Āhavamalladēva

e record begins with the Chāḷukya-*praśasti* and introduces the king Āhavamallad
s the conqueror of the Chōḷa armies. One of his subordinates or officers (name
ave made some gift to certain Mahēśvara Śakti-*paṇḍita* for feeding the ascetics.

TEXT

స్వస్తి సమస్త[-]
వనాశ్రయ
శ్రీ పృథ్వీ వ[ల్ల]
భమహా[-]
జాధి రాజ[- -]
రమేశ్వర[- -]
మ భట్టార [-]
సత్యాశ్ర[-]

9. [కు]ళ తిళక[ం -]
10. ళుక్యాభరణం

- - - - -

- - - - -

SECOND SIDE

1. [-]హా శబ్ద మహా మణ్డ
2. [- -] రం శౌర్య్యకణ్ఠీరవం [స్థా -]
3. [- -] న్తామణి సత్యరాధే
4. [- -]శౌచాంజనేయం భువ
5. [- -]రామ[ంస్వా]మిన[న్దా]
6. [- -]మన్త పక్షపాతి చో
7. [- -]మన్తబళ జళధి బ
8. [- -]నళచోళ కటక దల్లి
9. [- -]భయబ[శా] చార్య్య
10. [- - ర]ంగ ధీర శ్రీ మదాహ
11. వమల్లదేవర వగ్ఫ
12. శ్రీమన్మహామణ్డ

- - - - -

THIRD SIDE

1. తేంబుళ వా[-]
2. య నడు [-]
3. [శ్వరద] మహే
4. శ్వర శక్తి [ప]
5. ణ్డితర్గ్గె కాల[-]
6. కర్చ్చి ధారా పూ
7. ర్వ్వకంమాడి
8. యల్లియ

9. తపోధన గ్గాఱహో

0. ర దానక్కె సవ్యాఱ

1. భ్యన్తర సిద్ధి యా

- - - - -

- - - - -

SIDE

1. మిన్తి నిబరు [ం] రడిసువ రిద

2. క్కెఱ తప్పిదవగ్గెఱ బాణ రా

3. సి యొళ్ సాసిర బ్రాహ్మ

4. ణరుమం సాసిర కవిలె

5. యుమ నటిదపాతక[మక్కు]

6. సామాన్యోయం ధర్మ్మఱసే

7. తు నృఱపాణాం కాలే కాలే

8. పాళనీయో భవద్భిః స[వ్వాఱ]

- - - - -

- - - - -

No. 7

(A. R. No. 47 of 1969)

KARIMNAGAR

On a stone in the local museum

Ś. 913; Khara, Uttarāyaṇa and solar eclipse [**A.D. 992**, March 7, Monday
Western Chāḷukya
Āhavamalladēva

The record seems to be incomplete. It states that certain commander of th
ar, visited along with his army the temple of Mallikārjunadēva and endowed
l and a flower garden.

TEXT

IDE

1. ప్రచలిత రవి ఇ

2. న్దు మణ్డల మాకుం

3. చిత శేష ముచ్చల
4. ధీరు ధూ౯త సు[ట్టం]
5. భోరు భక రసులనం
6. జయతు[।]స్వస్తి శక
7. వష౯ ౯[౧]౩ నెయ
8. [ఖ] ర సంవత్సరం ప్రవి
9. త్తిసె ఆహవమల్ల దే
10. వంరాజ్యం గెయ్యుత్తిరె
11. తద్వరిష దుత్తరాయ
12. ణము [౦]సూయ్య౯గ్రహ
13. ణము [౦]దొరె కొశల ర
14. స లూ ర[గె]పాల మ
15. [-]రాల నీరు వచిన
16. [అపు దణ్డును]వారు

Second Side

17. య్యమల్లికాజ్జు౯న
18. దేవర దేగులమం
19. మాడిసి యదక్కె
20. ఖణ్డస్ఫరి[తద]
21. [-రణ] కన్దు [వి] దు[గ]
22. దల్లి మహాజన[ద]
23. [వి]యరె మత్త స్ని[౯]స్నే[౯]ం
24. నుం పుంవినతొణ్టముం
25. [పె]రెసలూర కిఱి[య-]
26. ంగవెయ[పె]తున[- -]
27. మహాజనద సా[- -]
28. [- -]కొట్టర చన్ద్రిశార

కం కిరుపల్లి [-]
[-] రదిం [-]పగెద్దె దె
ప్రయాగె బాణరాసి కు
రుక్షేత్ర మటిద పాప
కలయ్యం[ఖ]ణ్డరిసిద।

No. 8

(A.R. No. 295 of 1968)

CHOPPADANDI

On a stone at the place called Melakunta near the village
14; Nandaṇa, Śrāvaṇa śu. 2, Ādityavāra [A. D. 992, July 3; Sunday tallies with Śrā
ern Chāḷukya
vamalladēva
ie record registers the construction of the tank Āchebbe-*samudra*, named after Āc
of Anuṅgu Duggarayya the follower of Iṟivebeḍeṅga and the monetary gift of [70 .
y the latter's *dādi* Dēvakabbe.

TEXT

స్వస్తి సమస్తభువనాశ్ర
య శ్రీపృథ్వీ వల్లభ మ
హారాజాధిరాజ పర
మేశ్వర పరమభట్టా
రక చాళుక్యాభరణ
సత్యాశ్రయ కుళ
తిళకం శ్రీమ దా
హవమల్లదేవర రా
జ్యముత్తరోత్తరా
భి వృద్ధియి స్సాచ
న్ద్రార్క్కతారంబరం స
లుత్తుమిరె॥ శ్రీమత్

ౌళాళ [పుర] ర

రం [సత్యా] యుధి

ం స్వామి [నిబ్రిత్యం]

చ - - -]

ం [మి - తుం] విబు

ాశ్రయం బ

కల్పవృతం

వెడెంగ (శ్రీ)

ంగు దుగ్గర

ంగళ పిరియ

]ళాచబ్బగ

డ్ఢియో ళా

బ్బ] సము [ద్ర] మె[ంబ]

45. ఒం [- -]నెఱయెకొట్ట

46. [- -] యనగట్టి వల్లి

SIDE

47. బోవంగ బోడి బోడి

48. గ కెఱెయ పెఱగె [నీ]

49. రునేలంమత్త మూఱ[ప్ప]

50. [. ఱి]య నేల మత్తప్పఱ

51. న్నెరడు బ్రహ్మపురియ

52. పా [వ్వఱ] న్నా రణయ్యం [గె]

53. నీరు నేలం మత్త రొన్దు

54. కఱియ నేలంమత్త ప్పఱ

55. [న్నె]రడు॥ కన్ద [వ] శియప

56. శియప - - - -

57. - - గొమున్దుస

lines 58 to 69 illegible.

No. 9

(*A.R. No. 177 of 1966*)

JAMMIKUNTA

(*Huzurabad Taluk*)

Garuḍa-*stambha* in front of the Śiva tem

Tailapa II)

., Vaiśākha śu. 3, Aksha Tadige Śukravār

.e wet land and other lands and two *rāṭaṇ*
. village. Incidentally it mentions the kin
of the Paramāra kings).

TEXT

21. [illegible]
22. డెను గావుణ్డ నున్నా
23 గెయ [గావుణ్డనుందీ]
24. [ప వృ]త్తుమం[ని]ఱసి
25. దరు.

SIDE

1. స్వస్తి సకభూపాళ
2. కాలాబ్దంగ ళ్తొంభ[యి]
3. నూఱు పది [నేడనె]
4. యు మన్మథ సంవ
5. త్సరద వయ్యాస్ఖ సు
6. ద్ధ అతుతదిగెయుం సు
7. [క్ర]వారదన్దు దమ్మి[కుం]
8. ఔయ నాగెయగా
9. వుణ్డం తన్న[ఏ త్తిసిదు]
10. [త్రై లే]శ్వరక్క మాదిత్య
11. [illegible]

ళ్ల
థం ॥
ా ఖు
రాదిభిః
ుదా

No.10

KADPARTI

(*Karimnagar Taluk*)

Old stock

.su, Chaitra Śu. 5 Bṛihaspativāra [A.D. 1
'a
[Satyā]śraya
ı.

.ṁḍa - seven thousand and Kāḍipāḷu- se
ı and land. Doṇee's name not clear.

12. – – త్రైరో౦త్త

13. – – వ

14. – – జయ

15. – – య –

16. – బరంసు

17. – వి[నో౦]

D Side

18. దదిం రాజ్యంగె

19. య్యుత్తుమిరె రా

20. పుళ[కొ]ణియ

21. యాసనద బీ

22. డి నెళె సకవ

23. షణ ణాతిఃఇ నెయ

24. విశ్వావసు సంవ

25. త్సరద చైత్ర సు

ు - - —

జు కా

త్రైర డు - -

- య్యా-

దు — — -

సదె -

ర - -

ము

బా— —

ల్ల - -

ర

. -

-

ప్చయ్య

No. 11

(*A.R. No. 294 of 1968*)

CHOPPADANDI

(*Karimnagar Taluk*)

On a stone in the temple Śambhunigudi

iśākha śu.3, Ādityavāra [A.D. **1008**, Ap

id side of the epigraph is much abraded a

e gift of lands to the god Dīvakeśvara, s

village Choppaṁdyāṇḍi.

TEXT

కం శ్రీమ

ఏఱెఙంగ దే

దాది దీవకబ్బె [ం]

చా]ప్పందాౢణ్డి

ంశ్ మాడిసి

దీవకేశ్వరక్కె త]

abraded

హానోఽ్యయం ధఱ్మ్మ

ం న్రిఱపాణాం కా

ాళే పాళనీయో

ర్భిః సవ్వాఱనేతా

గినః పాఱ్థివేం

[ం]భూయో భూయో

HUSANABAD

(*Karimnagar Taluk*)

Old Stock

On a stone lying on the tank bund

ı missing.

TEXT

ɓ

ద

చా

డెుక్

హా

] శ్రా

పాతు.

No. 13

(A.R. No. 217 of 1970)

VEMULAVADA

(Sircilla Taluk)

n a stone set up near the Kēdārēśvara tem

a, Amāvāsya, Uttarāyaṇa saṅkrānti

[A. D. 1033, Dec. 24]

-hip and offerings of the god Rajaśvar

1. చంద్రార్క్కర్ తారంబరం సు
2. ఖ సంకథా వినోదదిం రా
3. జ్యం గెయ్యుత్తిరె సకవ

SIDE

4. శకవ ర్షంగ నె [ళ] శ్రీ
5. ముఖ సంవత్సర ద
6. పౌష్య దమవాస్యె [యా]
7. [ది]ను [త్త] రాయణ సం
8. క్రాంతి యం [దు వు - పు] రాణ
9. ద్రౌళి చీకరాజన మా
0. డిసిద రాజేశ్వరదేవ
1. గ్గర్ [న్దెళిచభా] గకుళుళా
2. [న] సహాస్ర [ద్రొళగె] సర్వ్వర్ నమ
3. స్య [చిదుగ] లనారావుతె

ర్యాదె ఆగ్నేయ దొశెనొ

ముంమూడలె సంకెయదా

బడగలె వెల్లేఱ సీమె దే

। శ్రీఖణ్డక్కం పుష్పక్కం

ఽక్కం పొఱలజెగ మా [శ్కృ]

। ప్రతిబద్ధద సూళి[య]

గ్మ్రా] నూర్వ్వ రనిబరెదివ గుత్త

। గె పరద రాఱు ద్రమ్మ సి

ము గుడ్లవంతెంక [డ్డె] దింగళి

। బెరసు నివెసనముం నూఱు

రగె తళభోగదనేలనె భు

[శ్లోకః] ధరామరకులేజాత

ర్వ్వ శాస్త్ర విశారదః వాజి

57. తత పలవుకాల నేలుత్తిరెల

58. వఱ్పాళగె [కం-] తరదొళ త

59. దంభోగం కొప్పర కొలకొరాయ

60. మఱిరెయె అల్లియ సిద్ధాయము

61. జెగవుం [ల్పా] పబగె మణ్డళేశ్వ

62. ర గణ్డయ్య జెగమం చక్రవర్త్తి

63. యల్లి పడెద పూర్వ్వ మర్య్యాదె

64. య సలసి బిట్ట కొప్పర కొల

65. సిద్ధాయక్కె దేవగుత్త పొల్లిరడ్డి

FOURTH SIDE

66. య మగం కొణ్డియరడ్డి

67. యదమక్కం [బీ] మ మ

68. [గ సోమరసె-ధర్మ్మ]

69. నిమిత్తమాగారెయగ

70. ణ్డని [ప] రదేవ పరివా

71. ర కామధేను కాయర

72. నెరవ[బ - - - -]

73. [హ్మణా] ధారం సోమేశ్వర

74. దసె పసాయిత[-]నమ

75. య్యం విన్నపంగెయ్దు శ్రీ

76. జయసింహ దేవదత్తి

77. యాగె కొప్పర కాల బి

78. ట్ట యమరాజేశ్వర ద

79. ఖణ్డస్ఫుటితనవకర్మ

80. క్కె పూర్వ్వమర్య్యాదెయ

81. సలిసి కొట్టొ [దిక్కిదు] శా

ాది

యుదా

తదా

No. 14

(A. No. 249 of 1972)

SANIGARAM

(Karimnagar Taluk)

stone set up near the Bhīmēśvara tem

rāyaṇa-*saṁkrānti* [A. D. 1051]

mahāsāmanta Kākatīya Bēta's *Pergaḍ*

aya of Saṇagara (village) and endowed it w

r named Muppaḍayya and Punniraḍḍi.

ed here is obviously Bēta I.

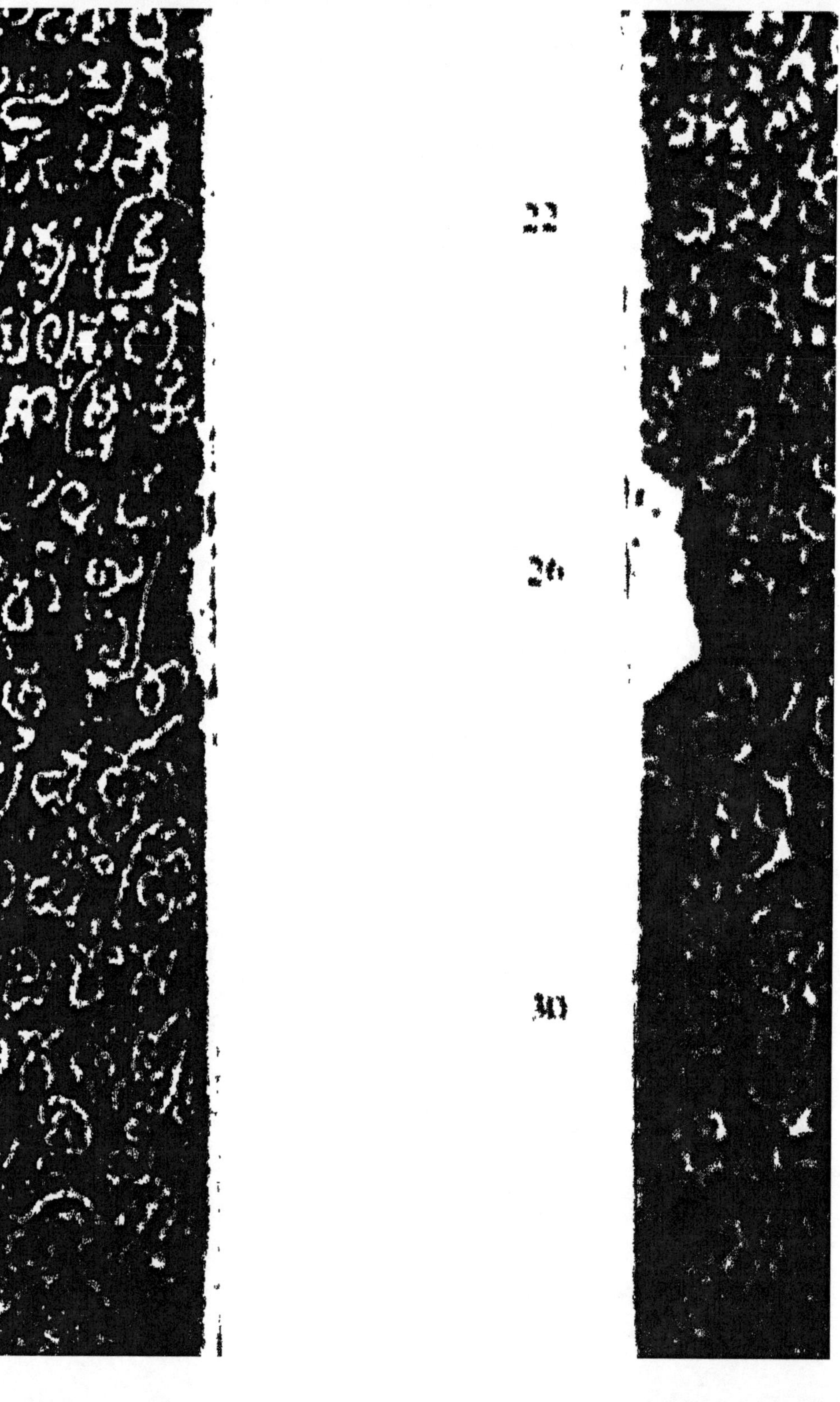

3. మాస మాచంద్రా

4. క్క౯తారంబరం స

5. లుత్తుమిరె తత్పా

6. ద పద్మోపజీవి

7. శ్రీ మన్మహా సా

SIDE

8. మస్త కాకతీయ

9. ఖేతరసరపెగ్గ౯

10. డె[వై జరాజన]

11. [మగణా] రణయ్య

12. [ర్] సకవష౯ ౧౨౩

13. [డె]సెయ విక్రుతి

14. సంవత్సర

15. దుత్త రాయ

]

].

No. 15

(*A. No. 312 of 1970*)

SANIGARAM

(*Karimnagar Tuluk*)

n a stone pillar in the field near the village

Amāvāsya, Ādityavāra [A.D. 1053, Nov

he king's subordinate *mahāsāmanta Kāka*
gift of twelve *maneya* of residential sites, a r

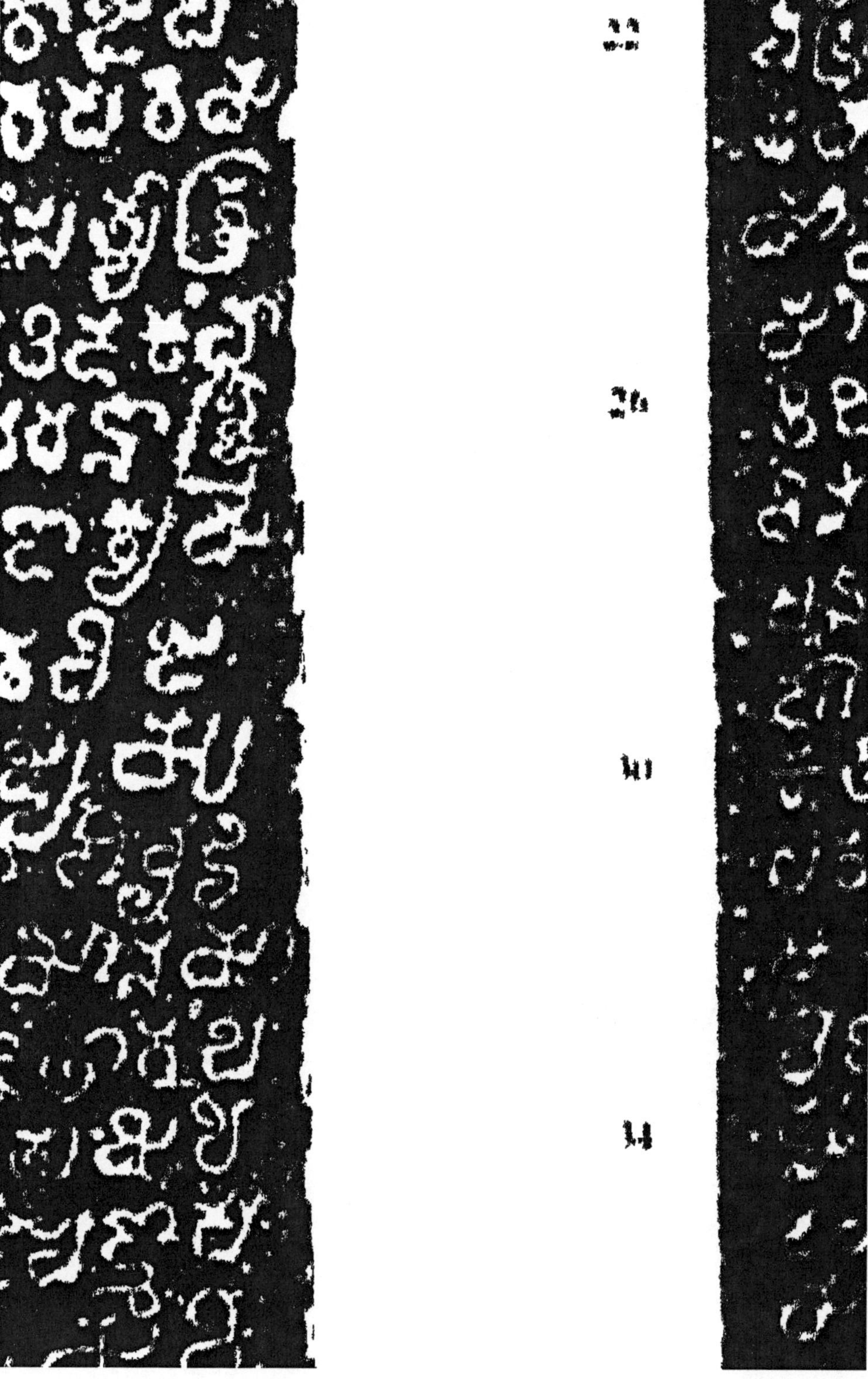

9. [illegible] ్యము

10. ల్లి దేవర విజ

1. యరాజ్యము

2. త్తరోత్తరాభివృద్ధి

3. ప్రవర్ధమాన మా

4. చంద్రార్క తారంబ

5. రం సలుత్తుమిరె

6. తత్పాద పద్మోప

7. జీవి సమధి

SIDE

8. గత పంచమహా

9. శబ్ద మహాసా

10. మంతం శ్రీమత్త్రై

1. లోక్యమల్ల వల్ల

కా త్రిక క

వా స్యాయు

త్యవార

సూర్యా

ణ పర్వ నిమి

ఖణ్డి సణ

ి శ వెగ్గె డె మ

ప్రయ్యంగ

ాడిసిద మ

పే]శ్వరక్క[ల్లి]య

ర్వగ పున్నె

ాపుణ్డానుమం

ప్రడయ్యగావు

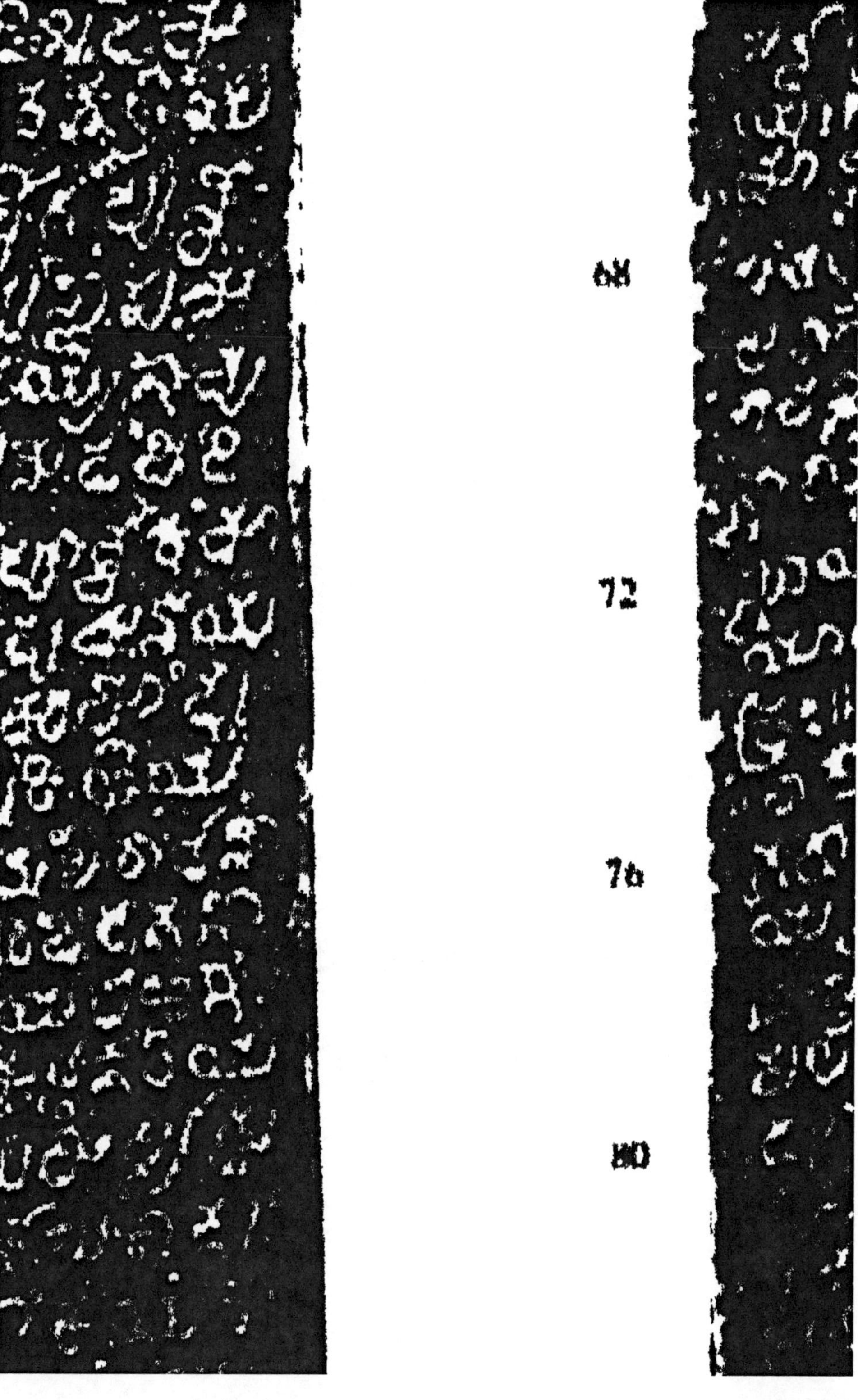

I Side

60. ము రడ్డియుం ప్రభు

61. నాగ రాజనుమ నొ

62. డంబడిసి పిరియ

63. దైణాంధు పెఱగో[ం]

64. దుష్ట్త నిర్న్నిర్న్నైలనుం

65. సర్వ్వాభ్యాంతర సిద్ధి

66. యాగ కొట్టర్ ॥ సా

67. మాన్యోయ న్ధర్మ్మ

68. సేతు ర్న్నృపాణాం కా

69. లే కాలే పాలనీయో

70. భవద్భిః । సర్వ్వానేతా

71. న్భావిన పార్త్థివేంద్రా

72. న్భూయో భూయో

73. యాచతే రామ భ

No. 16

(*A. No. 98 of 1974*)

POTLAPALLI

(*Karimnagar Taluk*)

On a stone lying in Rāmālaya

tra Pūrṇima, Sunday [A.D. 1066, March, 1

rāṭana (*mōṁṭa*) to a temple name not cle
on the occasion of the solar eclipse.

TEXT

ననాశ్రయ

ము

రమే

కం స

శకం చా

8. మా... లేంగో... ర్వాయ[వ][ం]

9 [ద]...వ్యరసర్... శవ

1. ... [ల] వెయ పరాభవ

2. ...ంవత్సరద చైత్ర ద పుం

3. ...వ ఆదిత్యవార

4. దండు సోమగ్రహాణ పర్వ

5. నిమిత్త దిం హాళైపల్లియ

6. నగరద పంచ మఠస్థాన

7. దం [- - -] పాధిష్టిత ద

Side

1. - ల్లియవక శ్వేర

2. దేవగ్గ...మల్లి [ప్పె] త

3. సాధన గ్గా...హార నిమిత్త

4. ర...ం[సుట్ట]ద ద్రవ్యాది స

ళం ॥

ధమ్మౄనసే

ాం కాళేకాళే

ఫ సవ్యా

es

No. 17

(A. R. No. 93 of 1970)

KORATLA

(Metpalli Taluk)

l in the old fort. One side built in the wal

'hālguna śu. 5, Bṛihaspativāra

s broken and letters are missing in each lin
enovation etc. to the Jinālaya probably by
u *goshṭhi* belonging to the Krāṇūr-*gaṇa* an

TEXT

14. రాన్న్య రాశిపిర్థిగా ప్ర
15. పర్థిగా పాగన మారవ [-]
16. ప్రాన్య్రగా గారం బరం ద [-]
17. ...రర వెలపి [-]
18. నాళ్ సుఖదిం రాజ్య [-]
19. ...న్యత్ర మిళు

SIDE B

1. ఫాల్గున శుద్ధ పంచ[- -]
2. [-]...వార దండు కొ[-]
3. [- - -ట్ట]న ...ట్టమాత్రణ్ణ జినాల
4. [- ం]...మత్సర్మణంది సి
5. [-]ఁ దేవరాదాయ్యఁ రాగె ప్ర
6. [- - -]యంమాడిసి గ్రహణ స
7. [- -]నాపుణ్యాతిథిమొళ్ ది

ద్ర ॥ క్రాణాగ్గణాం
తింత్రిణీ గచ్చు ॥ వళ
హా ఉంళిశె ॥ కౌరవ
ట్టు గోష్ఠి ధమ్మక్ష ప్రతి
పాళకరు ॥

No. 18

(*A. R. No. 172 of 1966*)

VEMULAVADA

(*Sircilla Taluk*)

On a slab set up before Rājarājēśvara temple

[illegible] V. 8; Rudhirōdgāri Uttarāyaṇa - *saṁkrānti*

[A. D. 1083, Dec. 25]

[illegible]stern Chāḷukya

[illegible]bhuvanamalladēva

[illegible] inscription begins with the *praśasti* of the king and his subordinate Mahamaṇḍalēśv[illegible] [illegible]atter is said to have defeated the Chiefs of Toṇḍamaṇḍala, burnt the forest fort of [K[illegible] [illegible] fame of Rājēndra Chōḷa, rooted out the Kurumbas, killed Vijayarāya Vijaya [illegible] [illegible]hōḷa country and the town Kāñchi. While administering the *Chabbi*-twenty - one [illegible] Kosavaḷa, one and a quarter lakh country from its capital Lembulavāḍa, he installe[illegible] [illegible]vara and built a lofty temple (for the same). With the permission of the king who was ru[illegible] Kalyāṇapura, he made some gifts of land and a village to the deity and for feeding th[illegible] [illegible]acher.

Text

శ్రీ శ్రీ శ్రీ శ్రీ నమస్తుంగ శిరశ్చుంబి చన్ద్రచా
మరచారవే త్రైలోక్య నగా
రంభ మూల స్తంభాయ [illegible]
స్వస్తి సమస్త [illegible]
[illegible]
[illegible]
[illegible]
[illegible]
[illegible]

10. న మజ్జజాణ్డ భవనం బ్రూమః కి మాతో వయం రాజాదిత్య నరేన్ద్ర కీర్త్తిలతా
11. త్రయవ్యాపినీ॥ కడువెడగాదు దెమ్మడగలాదుదెవిత్త మరాఠి సుం పడల్వాడి
12. పెడెగా [దు] దెంబ [చిదె] పొత్తిరలాద దెకయ్దు సత్యమన్నుడి వెడెగాదు దెం
13. సియలాదుదె నాలగెయెదు కీర్త్తి [పొ]ంగడి పిడె [రో]చిరలిసిద నాప్పిన్న
14. కూప్పిన సత్యదేగ్గెయం॥ ◎ స్వస్తి సమధిగత పంచ మహా
15. బ్ద మహామండ్డళేశ్వరం విరోధి మణ్డళికమదనమహేశ్వరం తోణ్డమణ్డళి
16. కమణ్డళి ఖాణ్డవ పాణ్డునన్దనం సుకవిపికనికరకోరకిత
17. సహకార నన్దనం నిజవిజయభుజాసిలతా నర్త్తకీనర్త్తన వినోదలావకం కుళిం
18. టాటవీదావపావకం రాజేన్ద్రచోళకీర్త్తివల్లీపల్లవనిదాహసమయదివసకరం వివే
రత్నాకరం
19. కుళుంబ కదంబనిర్మ్మూళనన[ప్పా]గదప్పదళనంవిజయరాయ
20. విజయసంహరణం గణ్డరాభరణం చోళకటకసూరెకారం పెర్మ్మాడియం
21. కకాలం కాంచీపురప్రబలబలపన్నగవైనతేయం వితరణవినోదరాధేయ వర
22. సక్కెకేసరి మణ్డళిక దిక్కరి ప్రచణ్డారిమణ్డళికమణి కృతాన్తం [కోయి]
23. యన హన్మ్మన్తనామాది సమస్త ప్రశస్తి సహితం శ్రీమన్మహా
24. మణ్డళేశ్వరం రాజాదిత్యరసర్ కొసవళసపలక్షెయ భాగము [మం] చళ్ళియిప్ప
25. త్తొందు సాసిరముమం దుష్టనిగ్రహ శిష్ట ప్రతిపాళనదిం పరిపాళిను[త్తు]ర
26. రాజధాని లెంబుళవాడెయ నెలెవీడి నోళ్ సుఖసంకథా వినోదదిం రాజ్యం
27. గెయ్యుత్తుమిద్దుజ శ్రీరాజాదిత్యేశ్వర దేవరం ప్రతిష్ఠెగెయ్దు మహోత్తుంగ శి
28. వాయతనమం మాడిసి రాజధాని కల్యాణపురద నెలెవీడి నోళ్
29. శ్రీమత్త్రిభువన మల్లదేవగ్గె బిన్నపంగెయ్దు కారుణ్యదిం దయగెయ్యె వర
30. శ్వర శక్తియాగి వరెదు శ్రీమచ్చాళుక్య విక్రమ కాలద ౮ నె
31. య రుధిరోద్గారి సంవత్సర దొళుత్తరాయణ సంక్రాన్తి నిమి
32. త్తమాగ దేవరంగభోగక్కం భోగక్కం దేగులద ఖణ్డస్ఫుటిత జీర్ణ్ణోద్ధార
33. క్కం [illegible] బెళియ కుళు మడు[వు]మం తపోధనర వి
34. [illegible] ఉపాధ్యాయర శి
35. [illegible] యుమం లెంబుళవా

ంయగటివృత్తియు రాజాదిత్య సముద్రద పెఱగెని తొన్దుగళ
రెటివు దెనితువం కొట్ట రస్థానక్కె భుజంగవళి కాళాముఖ [ం][నైష్ఠిక]
పోధనన నడెయసువం బ్రతచ్యుత నప్పవం [పా]క్కనప్పడరసం నగర పంచ
ుఠస్థానముం నొసలొ [శై] శ్వానపాదవనొత్తి పొఱమడిసి కటివరిధ
మ్మ్మమం ప్రతిపాళిసిదంగె వారణాసి యొళ్కోటి చతుర్వేదద పారగర్గె కోటి
విలెయం కొట్టఫల మక్కు మీధర్మ్మమ నళిదంగ నిబర్ బ్రా
హ్మణరుమ ననితె కవిలెయుమ నటిద దోషవక్కుం॥ ౹౹

ృత్తం॥ సామాన్యోయం ధర్మ్మసేతు నృపాణాం కాలే కాలే పాలనీయో భవద్భిః
ర్వ్వాన్ వేతా న్భావినః పార్త్థివేన్ద్రాన్ భూయో భూయో యాచతే రామచన్ద్రః॥
శ్లోక॥ స్వదత్తాం పరదత్తాం వా యోహరేత వసుంధరాం। షష్టిర్వ్వ
ష సహస్రాణి విష్టాయాం జాయతే కృమిః॥ బహుభి ర్వ్వసు
ధా దత్తా రాజభి స్సగరాదిభిః యస్య యస్య
యదా భూమి స్తస్య తస్య తదా ఫలం॥ శ్రీమన్మహా
మణ్డళేశ్వరం రాజాదిత్య దేవర స్వహస్తలిఖితం మంగళమ
హా శ్రీ శ్రీ శ్రీ శ్రీ

No. 19

(A. No. 22 of 1971)

SANIGARAM

(Karimnagar Taluk)

On a pillar in front of the old Śiva temple.

. 1022; (mistake for 1028) Vyaya, Māgha śu.15, Thursday; Lunar eclipse
A.D. 1107, January 10]
Western Chāḷukya
Tribhuvanamalladēva (Vikramāditya VI)

ntions the king's subordinate Mahāmaṇḍalēśvara Kākatīya Bētarasar and stat
a of Mahāmaṇḍalēśvara Jagaddēvarasar named Koṇḍamayya made a gift of a *rāṭa*
r the worship and offerings to the god Svayambhu Bhīmēśvaradēva of Baḷiya Sa
ulgunāru-70

tīya Bēta mentioned here is Bēta II and Jagaddēva is likely Paramāra Jagaddēva.

Text

ఁ

స్వస్తి సమస్త భువనాశ్రయ
శ్రీ ప్రిథ్వీ వల్లభ మహారాజా

3. ధిరాజ పరమేశ్వరం ప
4. రమ భట్టారకం సత్యాశ్రయ
5. కుళతిళకం చాళుక్యా
6. భరణం శ్రీమత్త్రిభు
7. వనమల్లదేవర విజ
8. యరాజ్య ముత్తరోత్తరా
9. భివృద్ధి ప్రవర్ద్ధమాన
10. మాచంద్రార్క్క తారంబ
11. రం సలుత్తమిరె తత్పా
12. ద పద్మోపజీవి సమ
13. ధిగత పంచమహాశ
14. బ్ద మహామండళేశ్వరం
15. న[మ్మ]కుండాపురవ
16. రేశ్వర[- -] మ[హాహే]
17. [- - -] పతిహిత చరి[- -]
18. [-] య విభూషణం[శ్రీ]
19. మన్మహామణ్డళేశ్వరం
20. కాకతీయ బేతరసర్

SECOND SIDE

21. సమస్త ప్రశస్త్యుపేత స
22. మధిగత పంచ మహా
23. శబ్దాళంకారాళంకృత
24. శ్రీమన్మహా మణ్డళే
25. శ్వరం జగద్దేవరావ
26. దండనాయకుల కొట్ట
27. మయ్యాం [illegible]
28. [illegible]
29. [illegible]

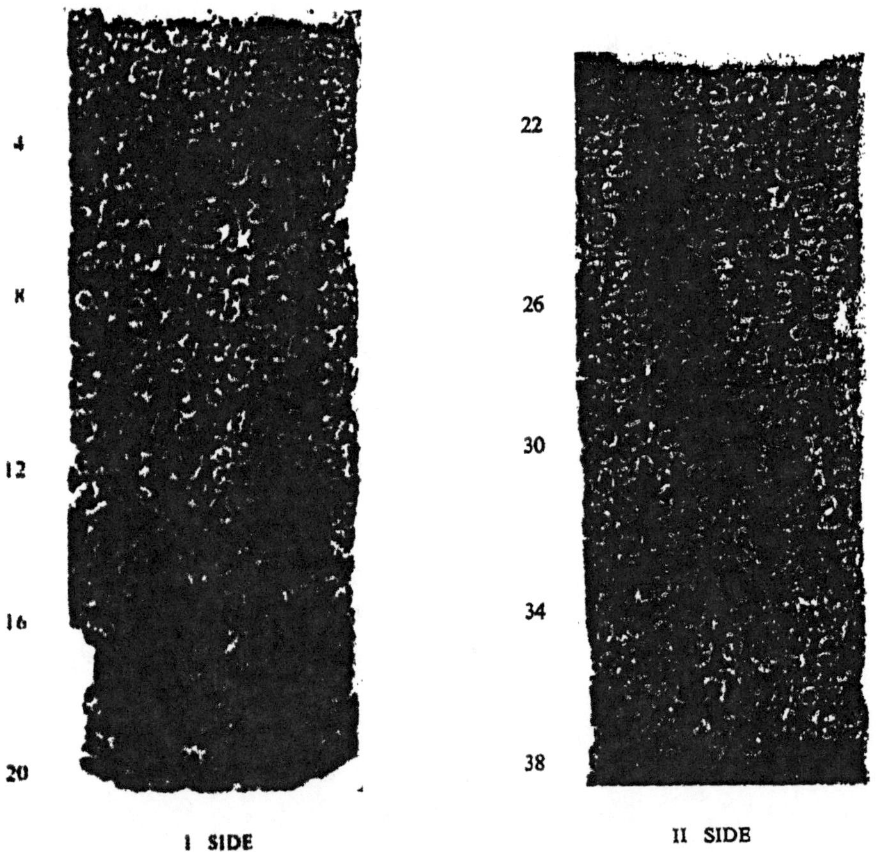

Ins. 19. Sanigaram Inscription of the Time of Tribhuvanamalladēva.
Kākatīya Bēta II.

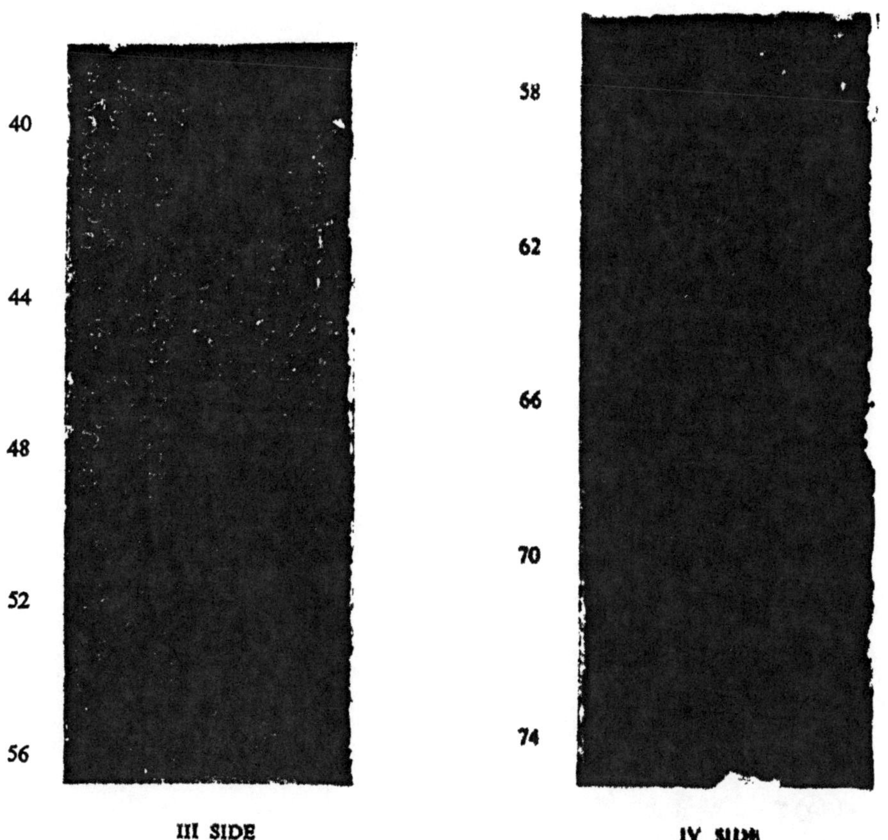

Ins. 19. Sanigaram Inscription of the Time of Tribhuvanamalladēva.
Kākatīya Bēta II.

. గురువార దన్దు సోమ

. గ్రహణ నిమిత్త మాగి

. ధారా పూర్వ్వకం మాడి

. పుల్గునూర ౩౦ ఱ ఐ

. ళియ సనగరద కళె

. యగావుండ న్మనొడం

ఐడిసి అల్లియ స్వ

. యంభు ఫిమేశ్వరదే

3. వగ్గేళ పూర్వ్వాదలు నడప

08

0. కాదెవ వరిగె యంబ

0. రాటణమం దేవర వ

. డువణ దెసెయ హెన్నెర

3. డు మత్తళ క్కాళరంబదె

3. య్యుం సర్వ్వబాధా ప

5. రిహారవాగి ప్రతి

5. పాళిసి ఖండ స్ఫుటిత

3. నవసుధా కర్మ్మక్కం దే

7. వర నివేద్యక్కం కొట్ట

3. ర్ ॥ సామాన్యోయం

9. ధర్మ్మక సేతుర్న్నృ పాణాం

0. కాలే కాలే పాలనీయో

1. భవద్భిః । సర్వ్వా నేతాన్

3. భావినః పార్థివేంద్రాన్

3. భూయో భూయో యా

4. చతే రామభద్రః ము

5. ద్వంశజాః పరమహీ ప

3. తి వంశజా [illegible]

H SIDE

57. పేత మనసో భువి
58. భావి భూపా యే పా
59. లయన్తి మమ ధర్మ్మ
60. మి [మ]ం సమస్తం తేషాం
61. మయా విరచితో ంజ
62. లి రేష మూర్ధ్ని ॥బహు
63. భి ర్వ్వసుధా దత్తా రా
64. జభి స్సగరాదిభిః య
65. స్య యస్య యదా భూ
66. మి స్తస్య తస్య త
67. దా ఫలం॥ స్వదత్తాం ప
68. రదత్తాం వా యో హరే
69. తు వసున్ధరా। షష్ఠి
70. ర్వ్వర్షసహస్రాణి
71. విష్టాయాం జాయతే
72. క్రిమిః ॥ దామరస
73. న బరహా మంగళ మ
74. వాః శ్రీ శ్రీ శ్రీ

No. 20

(A. No. 216 of 1970)

VEMULAVADA

On a stone near the Bhīmēśvara temple.

. V. 29; Vyaya, Vaiśākha śu. 1, Sōmavāra [A.D. 1106, April 10 Monday.]

estern Chāḷukya

ibhuvanamalla (Vikramāditya VI)

The inscription records the gift of a flower garden to the south of Lambulavā in the Venisāle seventy of Sabbi-one thousand, for the offerings and worship adēva and for the *achāri* who worships that god. It also mentions certain Māch maker of that garden. The gift was made by [illegible]

Text

)ః

1. స్వస్తి సమస్త భువనాశ్రయ
2. శ్రీప్రిథ్వీవల్లభం మహా రా
3. జాధి రాజ పరమేశ్వర పర
4. మ భట్టారకం సత్యాశ్రయ
5. కుళ తిళకం చాళుక్యా
6. భరణం శ్రీమత్రిభువనమ
7. ల్లదేవర విజయరాజ్య ము
8. త్తరోత్తరాభి వృద్ధిప్రవర్ద్ధ మా
9. న మాచంద్ర తారంబరం సలుత్త
10. మిరె శ్రీమతుకుమారం సోమేశ్వ
11. రదేవరు శ్రీమాతు బల్లవ::న
12. గ్గే విన్నపం గెయ్దు చాళుక్య
13. విక్రమగాలద ఎ౭ నెయ వెళ్గి
14. య సంవత్సరద చైశాఖ ము
15. ద్ద ౧ సోమవారదందు శ్రీమద
16. రికేశ్వర దేవరిగె నివేద్యక్కం

Side

17. ఆ దేవరం పూజిసువ ఆ
18. చారియగ్గెయం చంద్రార్కతా తా
19. రంబరం సర్వబాధా పరి
20. హార మాగి సోవనారు
21. భదిం సర్వసాటిర దొళగె బేడ
22. సాలె రమ్యక్షేత్ర [illegible]
23. గ్రహారం [illegible]
24. [illegible]
25. [illegible]

డియ లొ౦దు హువ్విన
తో౦టముమం హారిద[ప్వ౯]
థక్త్రియుం ధారా పూర్వకం[ం]
మాడికొట్ట। ఆ తో౦టద [మా]
లగాఱం మాచిగంగం [పెరిదు]
కారుణ్యాం గెయ్దు [దలెక్కి]
ధర్మ్మమం ప్రతిపాళిసిద
రీ ధర్మ్మమ నాళ్కియ రసరా
రాను ముపేక్షిసి దొడ షల్లి
యర్థోపేక్షయం మాడి దొడం
వారణాసియలు కోటి క
విలెయుమం కోటి విద్వాంసరు
మం కొ౦దపాప మక్కుం
స్వదత్తాం పరదత్తాం వా యో హ
రేతి వసుంధరాం షష్టి
వర్షసహస్రాణి వి
ష్ఠాయాం జాయతే క్రి
మిః ✢

No. 21

(A. No. 215 of 1970)

VEMULAVADA

On another stone set up near the Bhīmēśvara temple.

031; Sarvadhāri Vaiśākha śu. 14, Ādivāra [A. D. 1108, April 26, Sunday]

stern Chāḷukya

huvanamalla [Vikramāditya VI]

The inscription registers the gift of the place (village?) Illihindilumpa for the [illegible]adeva and the feeding of ascetics by *Mahāmaṇḍalēśvara* Jagaddēvarasar of Pāvāra [illegible]de into the hands of Bhīmēśvara Paṇḍita of Siṁgha Parișe.

TEXT

T SIDE

స్వస్తి శ్రీ లేంబులవాడ
సమావాస। సమస్త ప్రశస్తో
పేత సమధిగత పంచ మహా
శబ్దాళంకారాళంక్రిత శ్రీమ
న్మహామండళేశ్వరం పో
వార కుళతిళకం శ్రీమ [జ్జ]
గద్దేవ రవరు సకవర్ష ౧౦౩౧
నెయ వవ్వజాధారి సంవత్స
రద వైశాఖ సుద్ధ చతుర్ద్దశి
సి ఆదివారదందు హారికే
శ్వరదేవరిగె నివేద్యక్కం తపోధన
గ్గెఆహారదానక్కం సింఘువరిశె
బ్రహ్మేశ్వర పండితర కాలం కచ్చిఆ
ఇల్లింది కుంచెయం ధారాపూ
ర్వకం మాడి కొట్ట రిధమ్మనా మ[నా]
రా [ళి] యలు ఈధమ్మనా మనుపేళిసి
దదె వాణరాసియలు పాపిర క
విలెయుమం కొందపాతక
మక్కు॥

No. 22

(A. No. 248 of 1971)

SANIGARAM

(*Karimnagar Taluk*)

On a stone unearthed in a field near the hillock.

Ś. 1050; Kīlaka, Āśvayuja Amāvāsya, Ādityavāra; Solar eclipse [A.D. 1128,
Kīlaka and Ś 1050, but no eclipse]

Western Chāḷukya

Bhūlōkamalladēva

he record states that the king's subordinate Mahāmaṇḍalēśvara Kākatīya Poḷalaras
of Sabbi-sahasra (region) named Rāpola, Kuṃvarāja made a gift of one *ūpana*,

ds for the worship and offerings to the god Kommēśvaradēva of Khamdi Sana
ie ascetics.

TEXT

E

. స్వస్తి సమస్త భు
3. వనాశ్రయ శ్రీ
. ప్రిథ్వీవల్లభ మ
. హా రాజాధి రాజ
. పరమేశ్వర ప
. రమ భట్టారక
. సత్యాశ్రయ కుళ
తిలక[ం]
. చాలుక్యా భరణ శ్రీ
. మతు భులోకమ
. ల్లదేవ విజయ రాజ్య
. ముత్తరోత్తరాభివ్రిద్ధి
. ప్రవర్ద్ధమాన మా
. చంద్రార్క్క తారం స
లుత్తుమిరె తత్పా
దపద్మోపజీవి
త సమధిగత పంచ

B

మహా శబ్ది మహా మ[ం]
డళేశ్వర వస్నకుంద పు
ర వరేశ్వరం పరమ మా
హేశ్వరం పతిహిత చరి
తం వినయ విభూషణం
శ్రీమత్మహా మండళేశ్వ

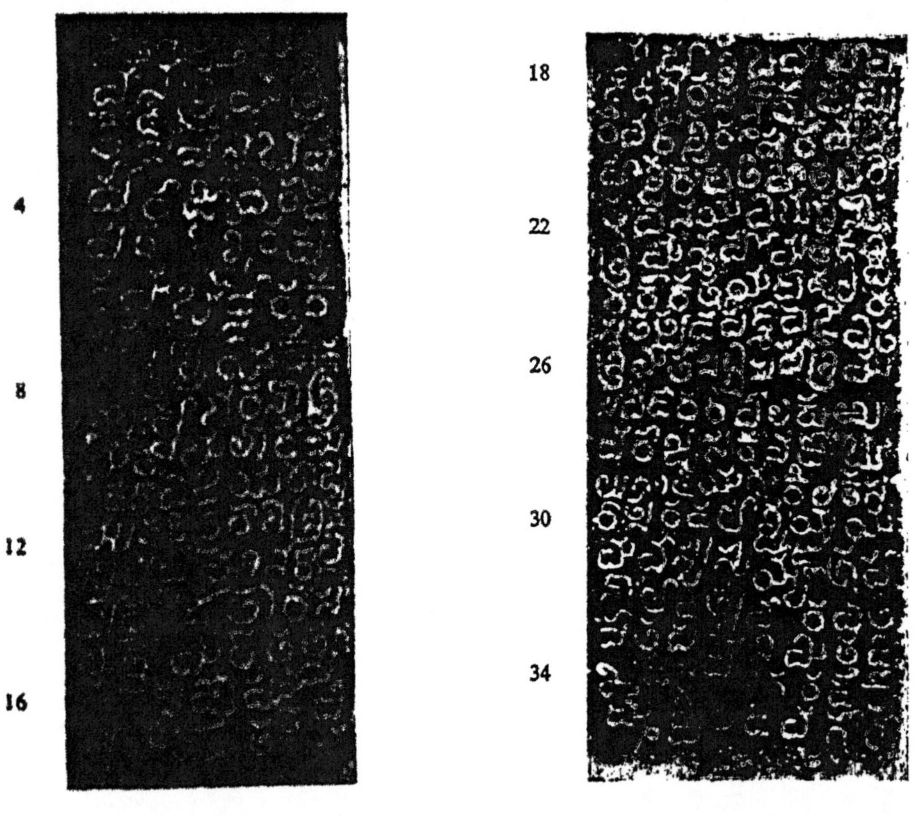

I SIDE   II SIDE

Ins. 22. Sanigaram Inscription of the Time of Bhūlōkamalladēva.
Kākatīya Prōla II.

24. రం కాకతయ పొళల ర
25. స న త్పాద పద్మోపజీవిత
26. (శ్రీ) మత్ సబ్బి సహస్రము
27. సవదొర రేచాల కుఱు
28. ప రాజు సకవసణంబు
29. లు ౧౦౩౦ యుగు శిలక సం
30. వత్పరద అశ్వయుజుయ
31. ముదాస్య సూర్యగ్రహ
32. ణ ఆదిత్యవార దెశ
33. పాత పర్వణ నిమిత్తదిం
34. ఖండి సవగరద కొ
35. మ్మేశ్వర దేవగ్గణంతో

IIIrd Side

36. కాశరద వండి
37. ఖ దేవగణం దీప
38. నివేద్యక్కం తకో
39. దవ రావొర క
40. వృద దావక్కం బ
41. మ్మద వరియ కొం
42. బ రాట్నద ళా ల
43. ల్లి మూడణ[హా ల్లి]
44. మత్త[ఇ]కణం కెరె
45. వాం కెయ బట్టియ
46. మూడణ కెరియ
47. మత్త[ర] కణం కెయుందు గా
48. ణద రాట్నద ఎడబు కల్ల
49. టు కొంగ బత్తబు కా

40. లు గచ్చిఁ ధారాపూర్వ్వఁక

41. మాడి కొట్టరు

SIDE

42. సామాన్యోయం దమ్మఁ

43. సేతున్రిపానాం కాలే కాలే

44. పాలనియో భవద్భిః సర్వ్వాఁ

45. న్యేతా న్భావిన ఖార్థిఁవేం

46. ద్రా న్భూయో భుయో యా

47. చతే రామభద్ర బహు

48. భి ర్వ్వఁసుధా దత్తా రాజభి స్స

49. గరాదిభిః యస్య యస్య ఎ

50. దా భూమి తస్య తస్య తదా ఫలం

51. కోటి పయకమలె పన్ని కో్కి [ఁ]

52. టి తపోధవర వేద ద్విజర పన్ని

53. కో్కటియసె కోటితీర్థఁది కో

54. టి మహాదిన దొలశిద ని

55. న్తిద వశిద ॥ స్వదత్తం పరద

56. త్తం వా ఓ హరేతు వ

57. సుదర శష్ఠివర్వ్వఁషఁ సహ

58. స్రాని విష్టాయాం

59. జాయతే క్రిమి ॥

No. 23

(*A. No. 288 of 1968*)

GANGAPURAM

(*Manthena Taluk*)

On a broken stone in the compound of the Āñjanēya temple.

Western Chāḷukya
Bhūlōkamalladēva

Fragmentary. It seems to state that a subordinate of the king named Guṇḍarāj[a] ... [bea]rs the title of *Chāḷukyarājya-mūla-stambha*, made a gift to the god Sūrēśvara ... [m]ay be identified with Mantheṇya Guṇḍa of the Palampet inscription and Guṇḍa of ... [in]scription of Rēcharla Rudra and Rudradēva respectively].

. ఋూరకులవార్ధిజ వ
. ర్ధన సుధాకరం శివ
. పాద శేఖరం ।[దా]కు
. త్య రాజ్య మూల స్తంభం
. శ్రీ మద్భూలోక మల్లి
. దేవ పాదపంకజ భ్ర
. మరం శ్రీమతు గుండె
. రాజులు శ్రీ మారే
. శ్వర దేవర[కు]నిచ్చిన

ID8

. [- - -] పంచమ
. శ స్థానములా కా
. రు వెలుంగ నిల్చి

ా న్యా

యూచ

ర్థాంవా

ఖన్డ

షఁసహా

ంజాయ

No. 24

(A. No. 17 of 1971)

SANIGARAM

(Karimnagar Taluk)

tone pillar set up near the Śiva temple in t

itra śu. 15 Thursday, lunar eclipse [A.D. 1

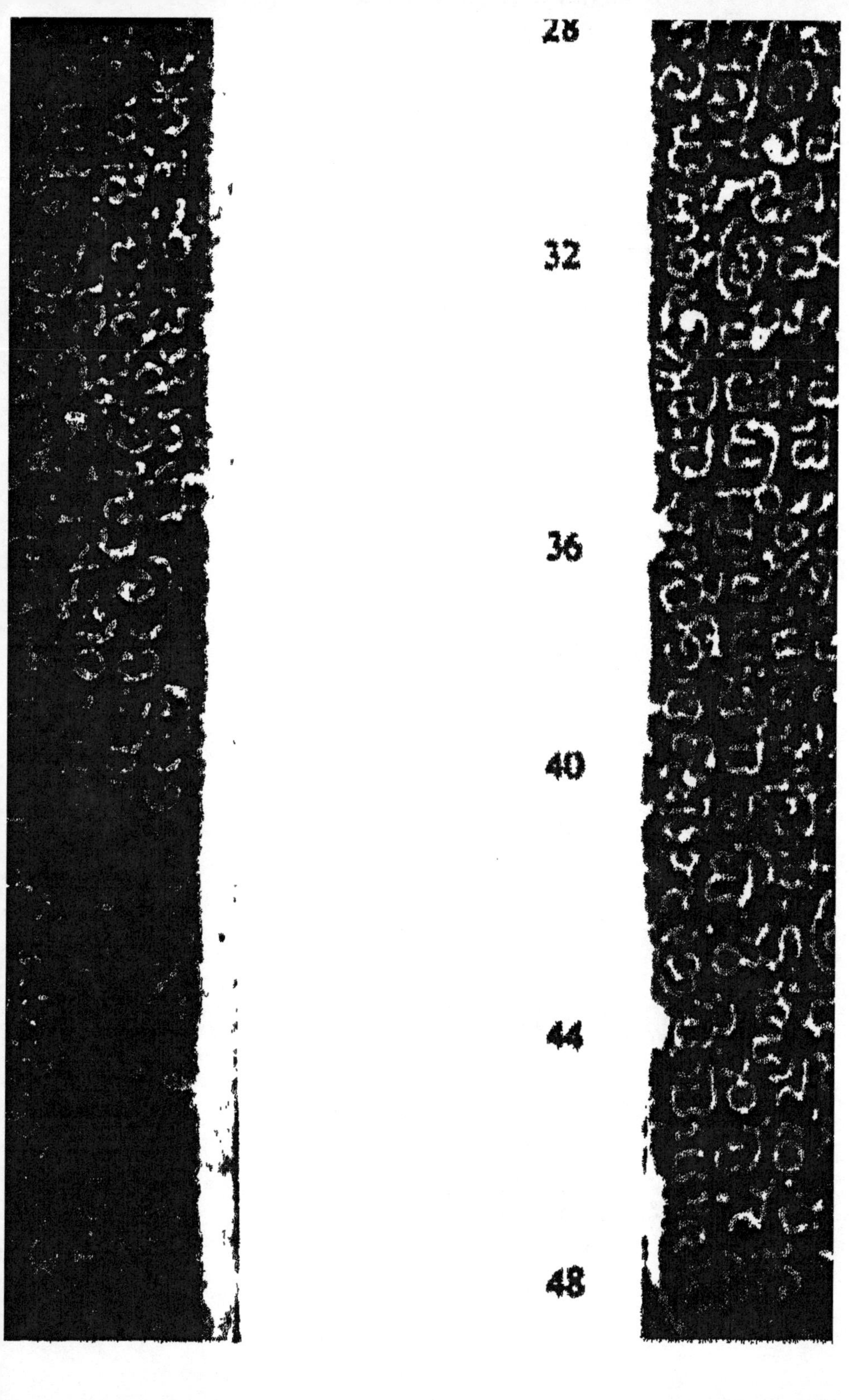

ల్ల బవ వఱు

రాజ్యముత్తరోత్తరా

భివృద్ధి ప్రవర్ధమా

న మాచంద్రార్క తా

రం సలుత్తుమిరె త

త్పాద పద్మోపజీవి

త సమధిగత

పంచ మహా శబ్ద మ

హా మండలేశ్వర న

న్మకుండాపురవరేశ్వ

రం పరమ మహేశ్వ

రం పతిహిత చరి

తం వినయ విభూషణం

శ్రీమన్మహామండ

లేశ్వరం కాకతయ

30. దేవ మహాదేవుగె కావ నా
31. మాది సమస్త ప్రసస్తి సహి
32. తం శ్రీమతు సఖిళసహ
33. శ్రము సవదొరరేఖొల
34. కుఱువరసరం తత్పాద
35. పద్మోపజీవిత సమ
36. స్తోపేత సమధిగత పంచ
37. మహాశబ్ద మహాసామం
38. తాధిపతి మహాప్రచం
39. డదండనాయకం వస్తుగు
40. ణ వస్తునాయకం కమ్మ
41. కులాభరణం యాశ్రిత జ
42. న పోషణం సుజన పవి
43. త్రం యాత్రేయ గోత్రం శ్రీ
44. మద్దండనాయకం మంత
45. పరసరు శ్రీపార్థేశ్వర
46. దేవరిగె నిత్యనివేద్య
47. క్కం నందాదీవిగెం త
48. పోధన ఆహార క

D Side

49. ప్పడ దానక్కం శక వ
50. ష౯ ౧౦౭౧ నెయ
51. శుక్ల నంవత్సరద చై
52. త్రసుద్ధ[౧]౫ యు గు
53. రు వారం విషు సంక్రాం
54. తి వ్యతీపాత సోమ
55. గ్రహణాధి పు[ర్వ౯]
56. కంనూ ఱొంబ రాటవం

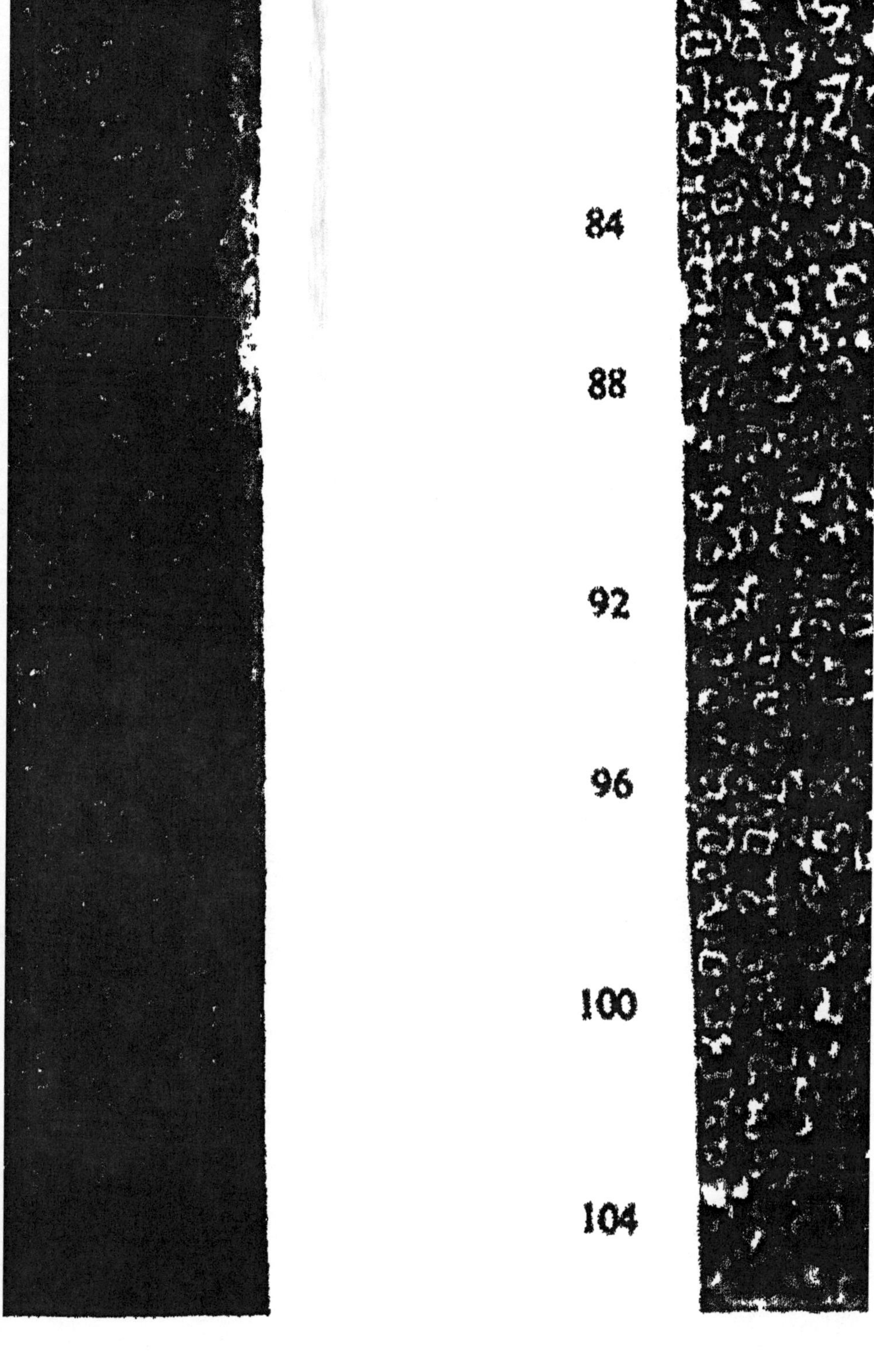

మం ఎం

త దేవ

ధా రా పూ

ొట్టరు ।

ద్రివ

మూ

థవ సం

[ల]ఖాగిరథి

రణ్య దేవ

త్రవిధి వ

యుర్యాన్ ।

మ్మర్గా

ం గా

ండూ[థ]

ంస్థత ॥ కో టా ప

్లకోటి తపో

ర]ం కో[ట]కోటి

త్థాది కోటి

ిద నింతి

త్తం పరదత్తం వా

యుంధరాం షష్టి

[ర్షాణి మిష్టాయాం

॥ చిత్ర పెలిలి

ముం కిడి[వె]

]దువరస్వా త్తి

శం య[న్తి] ?

ఘట

॥

నెమా [- -]

the *gotra* of Atri, Kommanārya was born. His son and grandson were respectively I
da. To Gōvinda and his wife Turukamāmbā was born Gaṁgādhara. After comp
Gaṁgādhara joined in the service of Kākati Prōla and became the minister of Rudra
cord registers the grant of Diṁḍoṁṭa village as *agrahāra* to the brāhmaṇas and the
ikūṭa temple to the god Śiva by Gaṁgādhara. He is also said to have constructed
ces, Anumakoṇḍa, Hiḍiṁbāchala, Nagarūru etc., the last named being the capital
which he was appointed as governor.

TEXT

1. శ్రీరామాధిపు డింద్రనీలనిభ శారీ
2. రుం డుదారుండు గౌరీరామాధి
3. పుం డుజ్వల స్ఫటిక శారీరుండు ధీరుండు
4. భాషా రామాధిపుం దక్షకేవరలవ
5. ద్యారీరుండుమం గారుణ్యాంబువ మా
6. కు నీవుత సదా శాలంబుం గావ్యాత్మకాము
7. లు[1*] వెలయుంగ వేంగిదేశంబులోన నా
8. త్రేయగోత్ర పుంగవులు మహాత్ములు
9. వెల్లిపురంబున అనవద్యులు పుట్టి పెరిగి
10. పాలించి చనము [2*] మనుచరితుం దశల [illegible]
11. గణన పూజితుం డైన యత్రిసంతానము
12. నను జనియించి కొమ్మనార్యుల్గాండు విను
13. త శ్రీ కుత సమృద్ధి వెలయుంగ [illegible]
14. వ[3*] [illegible]
15. వ్వయ [illegible]
16. నుం డుదియించె [illegible]
17. [illegible]
18. [illegible]
19. [illegible]
20. [illegible]
21. [illegible]
22. [illegible]

23. వితతయశుండైన యతనికిం బతివ్రతా
24. గుణవిభాసి భాగ్యవతి మహాసతి యైన
25. తురుకమాంబకు నుతచరితుండ బంధుజనము
26. నోముదకరుండను॥ [6*] వృత్త॥ భూధరధైర్యుఁ
27. నత్యధిక పుణ్యచరితుం డపారకీర్తిఁ లక్ష్మి
28. ధరమూర్తిఁ శిష్టజనమిత్రుండు గోత్ర ప
29. విత్రుం డచ్యుతారాధన తత్పరుండు న
30. రరాజగురుండు మతిప్రభాతి గంగాధ
31. రుం డిద్ధరిత్రి ననంగా నుదియించి శుభోదయం
32. బువన్॥ [7*] కంద॥ మాతాపిత్రు వర్గము సంప్రీ
33. తిం జదివించి మన్ని పెన్ని లసద్విద్యాతిశయ
34. కుశలుం జేసి విభూతిం బరిణయము
35. సేసి పోషింపంగాను॥ [8*] వృత్త॥ సకలకలావిధి
36. జ్ఞుం డనం జాలి సమస్త జనా[లి] సద్గుణ ప్రకర
37. మునెప్పుడును బుధసభం బ్రణుతింప
38. ంగ నున్నయట్టి వమం బ్రకటితకీర్తిఁ
39. ప్రోలజవపాలుండు ఘోరతరాజి
40. లోలుం డత్యకుటిల చిత్తుం డీతండని యాదరి
41. కం బిల్పించి వంపంగాన్॥ [9*] కంద॥ చనవుమె
42. యి నగరిలోం దగుపనులెల్లమం బెంపు
43. మెఱపి పరికించుచు సేప్పుడవ భక్తి యు
44. క్తి వతిముదమునం జేయుచుం దత్పరోక్ష
45. మున మఱియుం బ్రథము॥ [10*]

SECOND SIDE

46. (శ్రీ)కాన్తా కాన్తుతే [illegible]
47. [illegible] [*11]

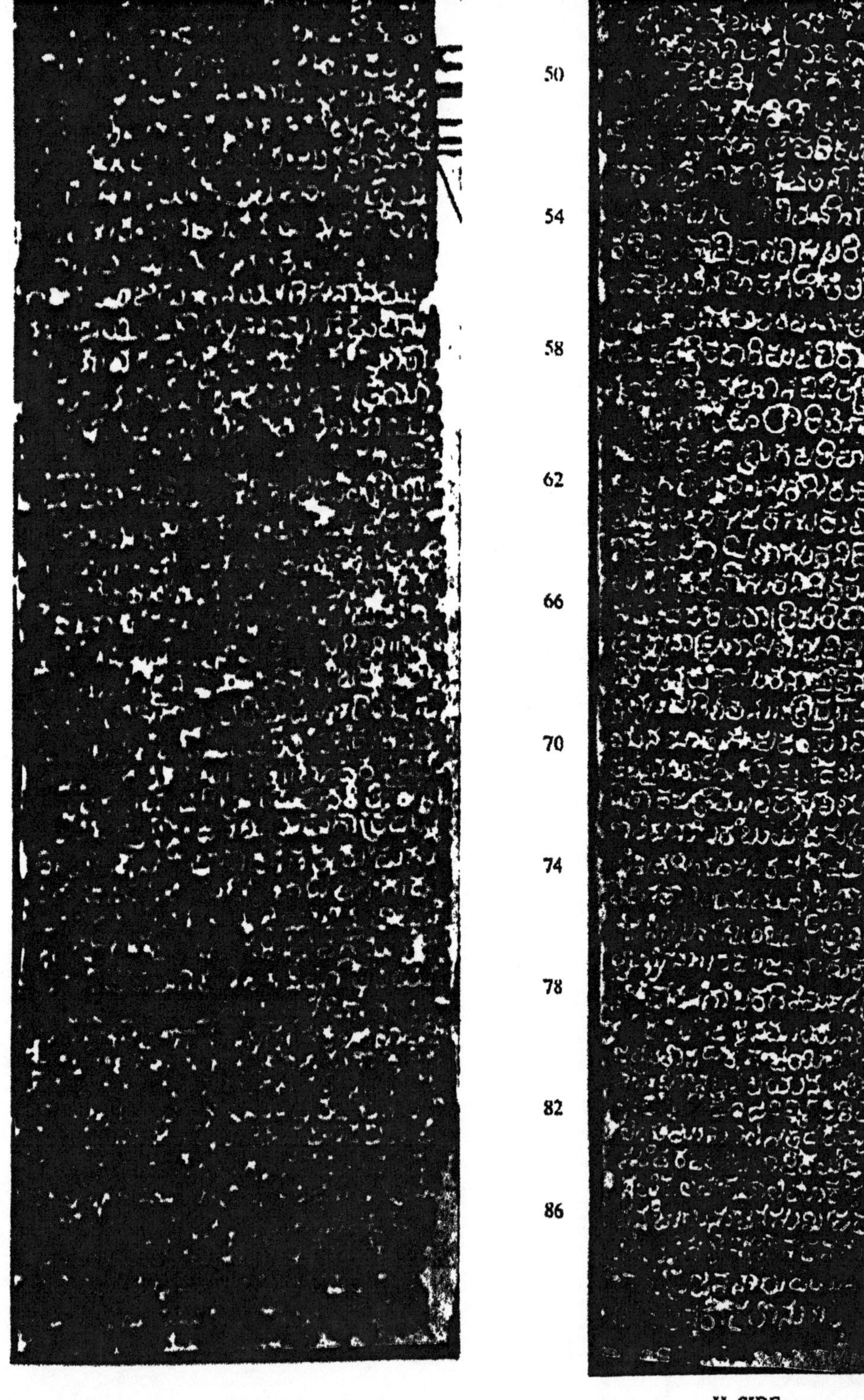

I SIDE

II SIDE

కాన్తా కాన్తుచే విస్త్రుత నిజ
భుజనిస్త్రింశనికాన్యరాజ శ్రీకా
న్తా కాన్తుచే దిశితి గగన స
మాశ్లిష్ట విస్పష్ట కీర్తి శ్రీకాన్తా
కాన్తుచే సూర్జితరిపుశ్రమి
గరాతిశ్రమిగారాతి చేతన్॥[11*] శ్రవి॥
పరమ్మపాల మౌలిమణి భాను
ర దీప్తిలతా వితాన విస్ఫురిత
పదాబ్జుచే నహిత భూతలవా
భవరూధినీ సరోవరమథనప్రభూ
త మదవద్వరదాధిపుచే విరోధి
భూధర శిఖర ప్రభిన్నవిదిత శ్రీ
దశేంద్రనికాశకేతిచేన్ [12*] ॥క॥
సురకరివర(తి)మృగపతి హరి
సురపతి దమల సరసీరుహా
కుక్షిరుహ సదృశ(కుచే)యురు చిర
విశద యశోశాసుర నిధిచే
సుకవి ధరణీసుర నిధిచేతన్॥ [13*]
పరనిధివరిత ధాత్రీ పరిపాలి
త దక్షిణ ప్రశాసి భుజవిస్తరు
చేత సబ్బికుండా పురవాభుండైన రు
ద్రభూపతి చేతను॥[14*]శ్రవిత్త॥ వెల
య సమాత్యసంపదయు విశ్రు
తమైన నియోగవృత్తు లందలము
శితాతపత్రము లశ్వ్యా విభూష
ణ శేపవాంబరంబులుం దగు వృత్తు
లుం బదుని భూమర వర్గముం ప్ర[illegible]
[illegible]

76. నర నిల్పుచుం బూజలు ప్రీతిం జ
77. ల్పుచున్ [15*] ॥కంద॥ జననాథు కరు
78. ణం దిండోం డనంగాంబరగిన మహోగ్ర
79. హారము విద్వజ్జనములకు నిచ్చి య
80. జ్ఞములొనరంగ జేయించి నా
81. మహోన్నతి వెలయను ॥[16*] వృత్త॥
82. అందుం ద్రికూటనిర్మ్మితశివా
83. లయమును విలసత్తటాకమును
84. సుందరపుష్పవాటికలుం బుట్టి
85. న లుంగలవంగశాల మాకంద
86. వనంబులును జనసుఖప్రద[మై]
87. వెలయంగం జేసి శ్రీనందనమూ
88. ర్తి రుద్రజననాథు దయను మ
89. టి యన్మకొండలోను [17*] ॥కంద॥

THIRD SIDE

90. శ్రీవిభుం బ్రసన్న కేశవదేవుం బురమధ్యము
91. న ప్రతిష్ఠిరముగ సద్భావన నా రుద్రే
92. శ్వరదేవు సమీపమున నిల్పితిం గడు
93. భక్తిని॥[18*] పుష్పేశ్వర దేవాలయ సాన్నిధ్య
94. మునందు కడుప్రసన్నతముగ
95. నప్పన్నగభూషణునకు సత్యున్నతిగు
96. డి నిల్పితిని మహోత్సవమునను॥[19*] పు
97. ష్కరనిధి పుష్కరరత్నము పుణ్యోత్తమమూ
98. ర్తి యన్నుబొగడంగ నను బుద్ధసరాము
99. తి వెలయంగా త్రైపురుషాలం జేసితిం బ్రతి
100. ష్ఠ పూజావారముగాను [20*]॥గంగాచియచె
101. బుధుసరెయిద్దం గేశవదేవు గుడియు

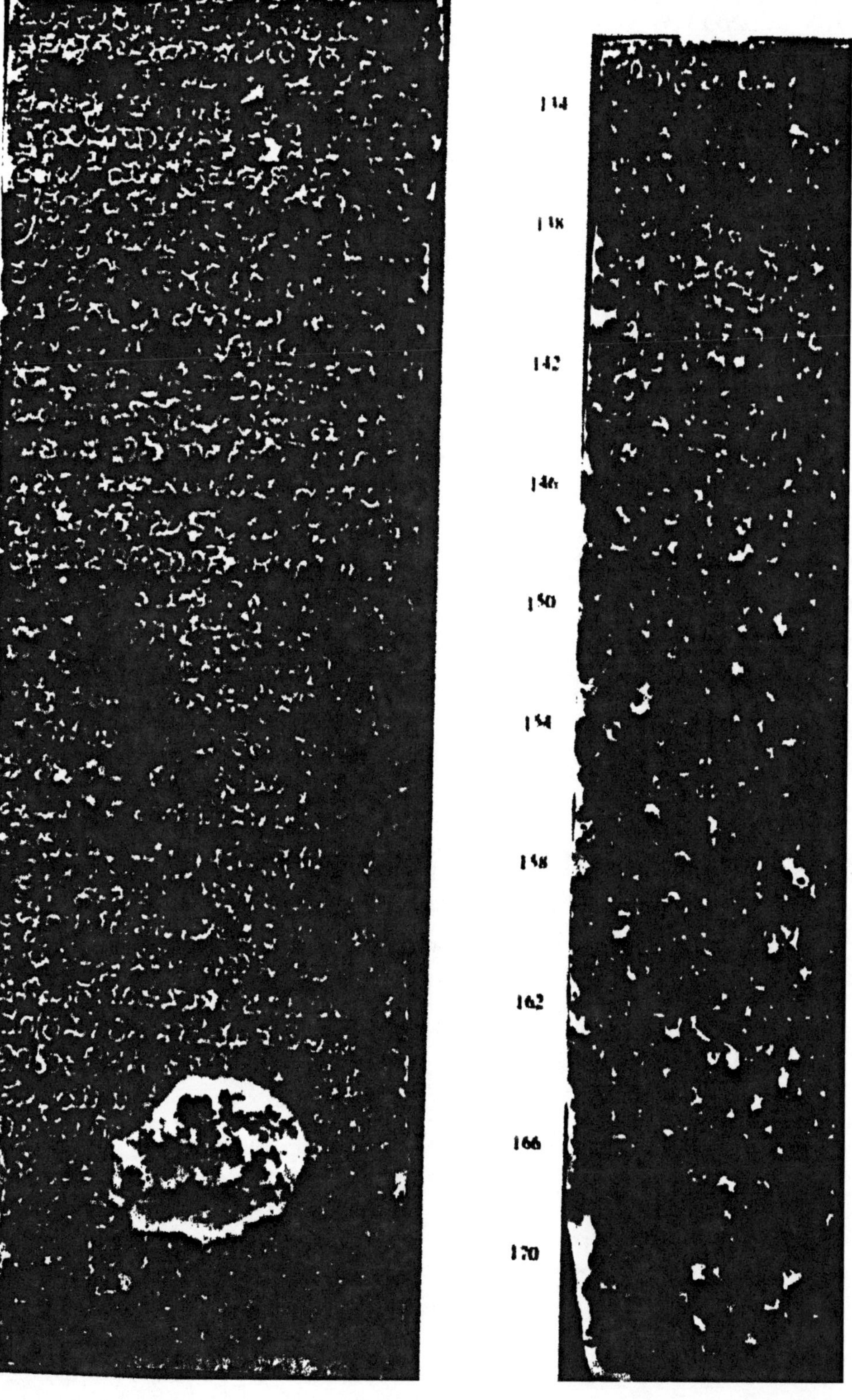

102. ధమ్మ్ర్గస్థితి తత్సంగతి విప్రులకును సంధ్యాం
103. గన గొలువంగ జనాశ్రయము
104. సేసితి నేన్॥[21*] ప్రి త్త॥ అంబుధివేష్టితావని
105. కి నాథకరం బగు నా హిడింబతీర్థ్గం
106. బునం బాదవోత్తము లుదాత్తమతు
107. లు మును భీమనాథగేహంబు మొద
108. ల్గం బెక్కు దివిజాలయములు సృజియిం
109. చి రేను భక్తిం బురోత్తమును హరి ప్రబ
110. తిష్ఠితుం జేసితి వాని సన్నిధిని॥[22*] క॥పర
111. మేశుండు హరి బుద్ధస్వరూపుండై యసుర
112. వరుల వంచించుట నా హరియనియ పట్టశా
113. లం జిరముగ బుద్ధ ప్రతిష్ఠ సేసితి భక్తిని॥[23*]
114. ప్రి త్త॥ ధర నత్యుత్తమమైన తీర్థ్గము శి
115. వ స్థానంబు సంవత్త్సరేశ్వర మంచును శశిఖం
116. డశేఖరుని విశ్వస్తుత్యుం బూజించి సుస్థిర
117. మై యుండం దటాకమును గుడియు నర్థిం
118. జేసి చేయించి యీశ్వరు సద్భక్తిం బ్రతిష్ఠసే
119. సితి జగద్వంద్యును భవానీపతిని॥[24*] కంద॥
120. ఎన్నంగం గోటిభవంబులం దన్నుం బ్రాపించుదు[ః]
121. క్రితములెల్లం జెడున్ భిన్నా సంగమ మా
122. డినంబన్నగ భూషణునిం జూడబడసిన
123. మాత్రను॥ [25*] అనునాదిమునుల వచనము
124. విని కాకతిరుద్రదేవవీరుండు విద్వజ్జన
125. ముల యనుగ్ర ...... ధమ్మ్గవు
126. నిల్పదలంచిద ...... [26*] ప్రి త్త॥ఆ
127. [కా]లేశ్వరదే[వ] ...... న్తతేజో[మ]
128. యంబై కైలా ...... మగుదేవా
129. గారమునిల్పి ...... ండొప్పం బ్రతిష్ఠ
130. సేసెం బరమేశును[త్తం – –]బు రుద్రేశ్వ

131. రును శ్రీకంఠును దశకంఠపూజిత
132. నిజ శ్రీపాదపంకరుహంబును ॥ [27*] కంద॥

FOURTH SIDE

133. ఆ రుద్రేశ్వరదేవాగార సమీ
134. పంబున[ం]దు గమనియ్యంబు
135. రాగారంబుసేసి నిల్పితి గారివ
136. ల్లభుం ద్రినేత్రుం గామాంగ
137. హరున్॥ [28*] తత్సన్నిధానమున
138. శ్రీవత్సాంకుం బ్రతిష్ఠసేసి
139. వలులంగ జెలు వం దుత్సవ
140. ముత్సోదం బెట్టి జగత్సుందర
141. కీర్తిఁ వెలయంగాం బరగి మహి
142. ని॥ [29*] వరమన్త్రకూటపురము
143. న వరదునకు జగజ్జనాభి
144. వందిత చరణాంబురుహు
145. న కాచంద్రార్కఁ స్థిరముగ గు
146. డ్డివిత్తి నిల్పితిం బ్రీణియు
147. నకుము ॥[30*] ప్రిత్త। కంకిత త
148. త్తియుక్తి సనిప(శ)ంబు విజాంధ్రము
149. లు గొల్పు వి[illegible]సంతము
150. ఖాఖల ప్రజవహాంధి
151. త పుణ్యపల్లవము ము
152. [illegible]
153. రు వద్యాను నీ తగ[illegible]
154. [illegible] మూర్తి [illegible]
155. [illegible]
156. [illegible] [31*] కంద॥

తన పెంచిన సన్తానముం దన
సన్తానంబుం గ్రితియుం దన న
ల్లిల్లును వనమునుం జెఱువును
గుడియునుం జనవినుతము
లైన సప్తసంతానంబులు॥[82॥]
స్వస్తి శ్రీ శకవరుశములు
౧౦౯౮ అగు విక్రితి సంవత్సర
మాఘ శుద్ధ పంచమి బు
ధవారమున శ్రీమన్మ
హామండలేశ్వర కాకతి
య రుద్రదేవరాజులు
నగరూరెక్కించి నగరూరు
[—]పలుగాము నచ్చినాండెల్లా
[ను]నముద్ధ[రింపుముని గం]
[గ]రాజున శిత్సు మంగళ......
[మా] శ్రీ శ్రీ

No. 26

(A. No. 188 of 1973)

MYDARAM

(Peddapalli Taluk)

On a broken stone lying near Chinnakondalrao's house.

Ś. 1098, Durmukha [A.D. 1175?]
Kākatiya
Rudradēva
Fragmentary.

The first side records a gift of land to the god Kēśavadēva and mentions the name ... iyaka. The second side gives the above date and mentions the temple of Trikūṭa in ... The third side mentions the name of Mahāmaṇḍalēśvara Kākata Rudradēva. The ... me gift to Prōlēśvaradēva. The contents of all the four sides have no connection with ...

TEXT

I

(a) [విక్రమ — —]
(b) కేశవదేవర

(c) వెలి[చేను]ఖ[-]

1. స్వస్తి శ్రీమతు బండి
2. బ్రమ్మె నాయకు[డు]
3. ...ముతూ

Incomplete

SECOND SIDE

1. శ్రీశకవర్ష
2. ములు ౧౦[౯౮] [అ]
3. గు దుమ్ముర్ఖ
4. సంవత్సర[ము]
5. [నా]డు మేడరా [జు]
6. ప్రతిష్టసేసి శ్రి
7. కూటము - - -
8. [శ్రీ మే...

Incomplete

THIRD SIDE

(a) [మఠ - ముా]

1. స్వస్తి సమస్త ప్ర
2. శస్తి సహితం
3. శ్రీ మన్మహా మ
4. ణ్డలేశ్వరం కాకెత
5. రుద్రదేవ రాజులు
6. ధమ్మర్థ ప్రతిపాలి
7. తుం చైన అనాది

Incomplete

FOURTH SIDE

1. ప్రాకేశ్వర
2. దేవరకు మ

తు ౧ లక్ష్మీశ్వ

ర దేవ - - -

Incomplete

No. 27

(*A. No. 244 of 1971*)

SUNDELLA

(*Peddapalli Taluk*)

On a Pillar in the field.

Ś. [- -]; Piṁgaḷa, Chaitra śu [8] Śukravāra [A.D. 1197, March 28, Friday]
Kākatīya
[Mahādēva ?]
Incomplete.

Mentions the king's subordinate (name not available).

TEXT

B

- - - - - -
[-] ధిగత పంచముహా - -
- - హా ముందరేశ్వరం అ -
- - - రాపుర వరేశ్వరం
- - - కేశ్వరం వశి
- - - తం వినయ విభూ
- - (శ్రీ) ముమ్మహా మం
- - ర కాకతీయ [మ -]
- - -దేవరాజులు ముల్లు నంక -
- దండుడ రాజ్యంబు చే[యు-]
చంగాం దదముమునం
[-వ]ర శకవరుషంబులు
- - - [illegible]
- - [illegible]
- - [illegible]
- - [illegible]

16. - - జ్జ మాంబకు నును -
17. - - చ్చిన సుపుత్రులు -
18. [- -త] దేవతాపూజాతత్ప
19. - - - హరహరచరణ

SECOND SIDE

1. బహుభి ర్వసుధా - - -
2. స్సగరాదిభిః । - - -
3. స్య యదా భూమి
4. తదాఫలం స్వదత్తా[- -]
5. - - - పుణ్యం పరదత్తాను
6. పరదత్తా పహా [- - -]
7. [- - -] నిఃఫలం భవేత్
8. - - రదత్తాం వా యో -
9. - - వసుంధరాం । షష్టి
10. - - సహస్రాణి విష్టా
11. - - యతే క్రిమిః ॥ త
12. - - హస్రాణి దేవాయ -
13. - పహస్రేణి దేవాయ
14. - కోటి ప్రదానేన -
15. -నశుధ్యతి ॥ - -
16. - - ॥డుమా - -
17. - - మధుకరుం - -
18. - - వాంఛితార్థకాము[భా]
19. - - టి [కు]ందు బయ్యవయి
20. - -॥

THIRD SIDE

- - యో భూ -
- - -యాదాశే
[illegible] మ -
[illegible] (శ్రీ) - -

No. 28

MANTHENA

On a pillar in the Hanuman temple near the tank called Tammacheruvu.

Ś. 1121: Siddhārthi, Makara-*sankrānti* [A.D. 1199, Dec. 26]

Kākatīya

Gaṇapatidēva

he record refers itself to the first regnal year of Kākatīya Gaṇapatidēva. A chie arāja, who was ruling over Chennūridēśa is stated to have made with the conse ıpatidēva, a grant of land to Manchibhaṭṭōpādyāya, the priest of the latter, the obj g to enable the donee to construct a village and a tank in it. The gift land is state ded by Gōdāvari on the south.

he donee Manchibhaṭṭōpādhyāya accordingly founded a village and excavated a tank gave house sites to brāhmaṇas of Mantrakūṭa. He also installed temples for Kēśav and gave a garden to the god Gōpījanavallabha of Mantrakūṭa.

Text

श्री मंत्रकूट गोपीजन-
वल्लभाय नमः । वंते निं
[घा] य हस्तं जयंति पिबतः
स्तमं गजमुखस्य । पुष्क-
रवारि तुषारा मातु भिन्न-
[कु] रेषु मौक्तिक विलासा : ।
[को]ल स्यकास्ति भुवनत्रयमू
लकंद [:] पाताल कर्दमिषु वा
धि जलेषु यस्मात् । स्वर्णाद्रि
केसर करालमराल दंष्ट्रा
नालं महीवलय मुत्पल मा
विरासीत् ॥ अस्ति प्रशस्ति शा
लि प्रवेशगृह मणिमवेशरत्ना
नां । अलकानुकारिविभवं वं[श]म-
हीनगर मोरुगल्लु रिति ॥
तत्र प्रकाशित धरणीं पूर्वो पी
नां इव गणपति र्नृपतिः । स

18. खिल नृपमौलिवलभीमणि
19. कि[र] ण तरंग रंगित पदा
20. ब्जः । पयोधि वेला रशना
21. [क] लापिनीं विधाय भूमी म-
22. [व] रोध भामिनीं दुकूल शु-
23. [भ्रै] रकरो द्यशो [भ] रै र्यं एष त-
24. [स्या] जवनी तिरस्क्रियां। तस्य
25. [श्रौ] तस्मार्त वीथ्यां रंधीति च
26. [ध] र्माचार्यकं अंचनार्यः
27. [स्व म] हिम्ना सर्वे विधासु ...
28. ... ...
29. ... ...
30. ... ...

SECOND SIDE

1. [म] धुरंलिभंग्या महः [प्रति]-
2. [ष्ठा]प्य रमासहायं । नि[जा]-
3. भिधेये निगमांत वार्त्ता[-]
4. [त्ता] मिदंता परता मनैषीत् ॥
5. [प्रा] साद मप्यकल्पय दात्म य[शो]
6. राशिकल्प माकल्पं । यत्कनक
7. कलश कांत्या संध्यारुण इव [न]-
8. भोंतरे पि रविः ॥ सुरिलि मंणिभि
9. रत्नप्रकाशया कृष्णनायक स
10. नाथया [च] यः । सौधपालि न-
11. वमौक्तिक स्रजा मंलकूट नग-
12. री मभूषयत् ॥ जनितो यकक्मा
13. बायां तेन श्रीमल्लिकार्जुनः । कश्य
14. [पे]न य यादित्यां तेजसा भास्करो
15. [र]विः ॥ कस्य समस्ति दिव्यी धन

[- - -] मल्लिकार्जुन बुधस्य ।
[- - -] नरपतीनां कथयितु मा
[- र्णा] केवलं शृणुमः ।। अद्वैतवि त्स
[ए] को न केवलं मल्लिकार्जुन बु [- -]
[-] त्यागे तं कलयंतः सर्वे प्यद्वै -
[तवा] दिनो भुवने ।। अनुज स्य केशव [सू]
[रिः] कर्मसु धर्मेषु तेष तेषु मुदा [-]
[-] मेव प्रतिबिंब स्तस्य गरीया नसम
[व] तिष्ट ।। प्रेम्ना प्राणुपलालना [थं]
[म] बितु भूमीभुजा लालितो वा [- - -]
[-] विनीतवाग्विभवनः प्राज्या [- - -]
गात् । प्रत्यंगाभरणा[यं - -]
[- - -]स्ततद्भुजा [संश्रितः - - -]
- - - - - - -
- - - - - - -
- - - - - - -

DB

ना कल्लोलितकरुणकर वाल सुरभित [illegible]-
[तः] सौमित्रि रिव रघुपते रनुजन्मा
[गोपालः] : कवि [illegible] ।। [illegible] (डे) प[illegible]
[ष्का] धनाचार्य [illegible]
हारताणुमत्या [illegible] [प]
धर्मजलिना [illegible]
[दें] व महाराज [illegible]
[illegible] नि[षि] [illegible]
[illegible]
[illegible]

11. र्तमानेषु सिद्धार्थि संवत्सर (रे) मकर
12. संक्रांतिकाले गोदावरी प्प्रणीता-
13. संङ्गमे शक वर्षेषु देशो दत्तः [।*][त]स्य
14. सीमानः पूर्वतो वेनकेपंडिः दक्षि-
15. णतो गोदावरी पश्चिमतः अय्य-
16 नव्रोलि तटाक उत्तरतः पुञ्चकाय[ल]-
17. वेगिलिः [।*] तस्मि न्देशे मंचे(च) [नार्ये]
18. ण तटाक ग्रामौ रचयित्वा ब्रा[ह्म]
19. णेभ्यो मंत्रकूटवाटिका वासि[भ्य]-
20. श्च स्वकुटुम्बाय च दत्तौ [।*]तत्र महा[देव]
21. केशव प्रतिष्ठा कृता[।*]मंत्रकूट गो[पी]
22. जनवल्ल [भाय] आरामश्च दत्त[:।*]
23. तो मल्लिकार्जुन सूरे र्धर्मः मं[त्रकू]
24. टे (ट) गोपीनाथाय नागवुरे [तटा]-
25. कं अंगलूरे एकं [निव] र्तनं [मा-]
26. नपड़ि तटाके त्रीणि सह[स्र भा]
27. ग परिसरे यावनाल [क्षे] त्रं सप्त [ह]
28. ले(ल) परिमितं गाड्लुरुव्रुरे दत्त[द]
29. त्तानि [।*] काकतीय्य गणपतिदे [वम]
30. हाराजानुमत्या अल्लंबो [ब्राज]
31. दौहित्रा च्चेर्नूरि देश पालकात् [सोमे]
32. श्वरदेवात् मल्लिकार्जुन ... ...
33. ... ...

FOURTH SIDE

1. उत्तरतो गुंड़िवांगु : [।*] तत्र शिवलिं[ङ्ग]
2. प्रतिष्ठा च कृता [।*] तस्मि न्नेव समये स

[-]ल ब्राह्मणेभ्य: कोटपल्लि सं

[शा] कं ग्रामं क्रीत्वा तस्य मल्लिकार्जुन[पु]

र मिति नाम कृत्वा तटाकं च निर्माय [ब्रा] . . . .

[ह्म]णेभ्य: स्वकुटुंबा(बा) य च पुरतटाके द [त्तौ]

मल्लिकार्जुन पु[र]स्य सीमान: पूर्व्वं

त: पोतकुलु: द[क्षि]णत: कट्टंदल: प

श्चिमतो मद्दिकुंटवांगु: उत्तरत: प्रेग

ड़पल्लिवांगु: [।*] तत्र गणपतीश्वर प्रति

ष्ठा च कृता [।*] जोंनगामे श्रीलक्ष्मी[ना]-

रायण प्रतिष्ठा[कृता*] ब्राह्मण वाटि[का]

च दत्ता [।*] तदनुजेन केशव सूरिणा

अंबनारायण प्रतिष्ठा कृता [।*] म

ल्लिकार्जुनबुधसुतेन गोपाल

सूरिणा काकतीय्य [य] रुद्रदेव महा[रा]

जा नृमंतकूटे क्षेत्रं प्रतिग्रह्य त[त्र]

सिंहगिरिपुरं त[टा]क द्वयं च नि

र्माय श्री नृसिंहं प्रतिष्ठाप्य विंशति[गृ]

[हा]णि रचयित्वा तद्गृह वासिभ्यो ब्राह्म

णेभ्य: मंथेम्नकालुव एड्लपल्लि विलास बु

र चिरिपट्लु मल्लवल्लि कामिशेट्टिप

ल्लि अंगड़ी (डी) दु गुंजपड़ग नागवुर मं

स्ताल उप्पट्ल [म] ड़िकुड़ेपु पंचोत्त[रं]

[पंचतुर्सि] हगिरिपुरस्य [प] श्चिमत:

यावनाल माचाला चिचिति क्ष दत्ता [।*]

नरसिंह(ह) देवाय पुरा स्तूर्वत: तटा

कं बध्वि[द्वा] कुंटरूप[।*]लायपाल्या एकं विन

तंनं । श्री गोपीजनवल्लभाय तो

रेडिपल्लिगुंबबुरयो द्वे पुरौ [।*] विभा

ल ग्रामे एकं निवर्तनं । मुंमनिवा

32. कोसमेपल्लि मंथेनकालुव पच्लप
33. ल्लीषु अष्टौ [निवर्तनानि] [।*] उमाम
34. ... ...

No. 29

(*A. No. 141/A of 1971*)

KATAKURU

(*Huzurabad Taluk*)

On a stone set up in the Śiva temple near the village.

Ś. 1124, Dundubhi, ...7, [A.D. 1202]

Kākatīya
Gaṇapatidēva

It gives a lengthy genealogy of the Viriyāla chiefs, beginning with Sūra. Hi alla and Bēta. Bēta in turn had four sons named Sūra, Malla, Prōla and Kom em, had a son called Annaya, whose daughter Mailama married Chaunda of tl annaya of this family had a son Sabbaya to whom was born a son called Kāṭayā ƒtarāju and Chaunda - *sēnānī*.

The inscription records the construction of two temples to the gods Mṛiḍa (Śiv ıra by Sūra son of Bēta and further it describes a campaign in which Chaunda ımmand of Kākatīya Gaṇapati and defeated the Chōḷa king and earned the title *divi-c* stated to have constructed temples to the god Śiva and endowed the same with tax nealogies of these chiefs mentioned in this inscription are as follows :—

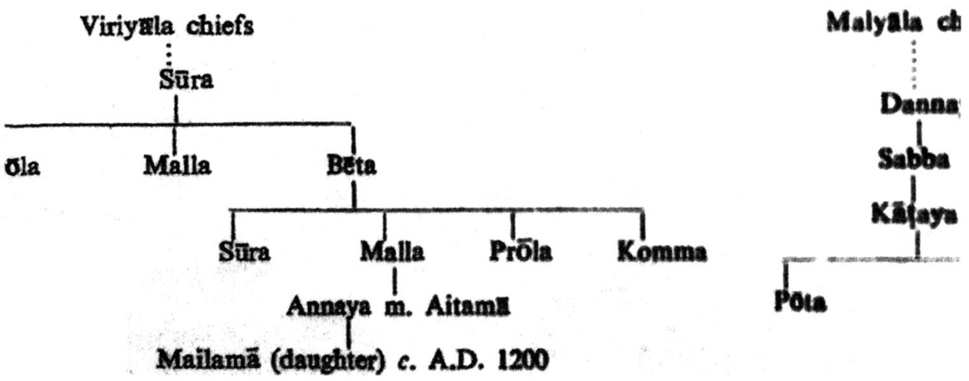

DI

1. శ్రీ ఓం నమశ్శివాయ। దేయా ద్దిష్టం గ
2. ణేశో వః ప్రారంభే నతమూర్ద్ధ
3 సు। పౌష్కరాః శీకరా యస్య భజంత్యాచార
4. లాజతాం॥ శ్రీమద్వరాహ వపుషః పురు
5. షోత్తమస్య దంష్ట్రాగ్ర వసుధాంచ్ఛలికా
6. చకాస్తి। పాత్వా హిరణ్యా నయనం జలధౌ నిలీ
7. న ముత్తస్థుషః ప్రథిత విక్రమ వైజయం
8. తీః భూయా ద్వః ప్రీతయే శంభు స్తాండవే
9. యస్య తన్వతే। ఉచ్చల జ్జాహ్నవీ వారా ముత్క
10. రా శ్శ్రమరశ్రియం॥ వరగుణ విరియా
11. ల జ్జాతభుజా మస్తి శస్తం కుల మమల మి
12. లాయాం యత్ర మిత్ర ప్రభావాః। అజ
13. నిషత మహీశాః శారదేందు ప్రకాశైః ప్ర
14. చురతర యశోభిః పూరితాశాంతరాళాః॥
15. ప్రణతిముదితశర్వాణః ప్రశ్రయతున్నగ
16. ర్వాణః పరహిత కృతదీక్షాః ప్రాజ్ఞలోకా ర్త్త
17. శిక్షాః। వితరణజితకర్ణాః విశ్వ కల్యాణ
18. పూర్ణాః స్సమర ది(జి)త నవశ్రా స్సాధు సిద్ధి
19. ప్రయత్నా॥ తదన్వయే జాయత సూరనా
20. మా మహీపతిః శూర జనస్య సీమా। య
21. స్య ప్రతాపానలతప్తగాత్రా భేజు గ్గుహాశ్శై
22. వారి వనా న్యమిత్రాః॥ యదాహవే వీరన
23. రేంద్ర ధనుష్కరే శరప్రలూనారి శిరస్సమా
24. వృతే। పలాయనా ద్భీమన్యపేణ రక్షితః క
25. థంచి దాత్మా తృణ జీవితాశయా॥ తత
26. త్రిలోకి తిలకా స్తనూజా స్త్రయ స్త్రివర్గ

27. ప్రతిమావతారాః। ప్రజజ్ఞిరే ప్రోలనృపాల

28. మల్లభూవల్లభౌ బేతమహీపతి శ్చ॥ తత్ర

29. బేతావనీశస్య సూరమల్ల క్షమాపతేః। ప్రోల కొ

30. మ్మమహీ నాథౌ చత్వారః సూనవో భవన్॥ తత్ర

31. [సూ]రనృపతి ర్మహోబలస్పష్ట మయ్యాన పురే

32. మృడాలయం। నిర్మమే సహరిభాస్కరాల

33. యం భూరివారి చ తడాగ ముత్తమం॥

34. తేషు ద్వితీయోపి గుణై ర్నృపాలః స మల్లనామా

35. భవ దద్వితీయః। యస్యాంగ లావణ్య బలా

36. దనంగః కృత్యం జహౌ పంచశర ప్రపంచం॥

37. స్నేహానిర్భర మగాధతా మలం సేతుభేదన

38. విధేః పరాఙ్ముఖం। రాజహంస రమణీయ్య

39. మాబభౌ యత్తడాగ మపి యస్య మానసం॥

40. తస్యా భవ న్మహోబాహు రన్నయః క్ష్మాభృతాం

41. వరః। తనయ స్స నయాచారః శూర శ్చా

42. రు గుణాకరః॥ తస్యాసీ దైతమానామ మా

43. నినీ నిజగేహినీ। రతి ర్మనో భవస్యేవ సాగర

44. స్యేవ జాహ్నవీ॥ విద్యేవ కీర్త్తిరం గురు సంప్రదాయా

45. దుద్యోగతో నీతి రివార్ద్ధ సిద్ధిం। సాలక్ష్మి పత్యు స్త

46. నయాం కులస్య భూషాయమాణా మథ మై

47. లమాఖ్యాం॥ మందసుందర గతం సుభా

48. షితం లోచనాంచల విలోలవీక్షితం। హంస

49. కోకిలమృగైః పృథక్కృతం యత్ర యోగ మ

50. గమ త్పరస్పరం॥

SECOND SIDE

51. యా సా వంఘ్రిసరోరుహా ప్రతిపదం వే

52. ల్లి ద్భు[జా] వల్లికా సుస్నిగ్ధాధరపల్లవా స్మితద

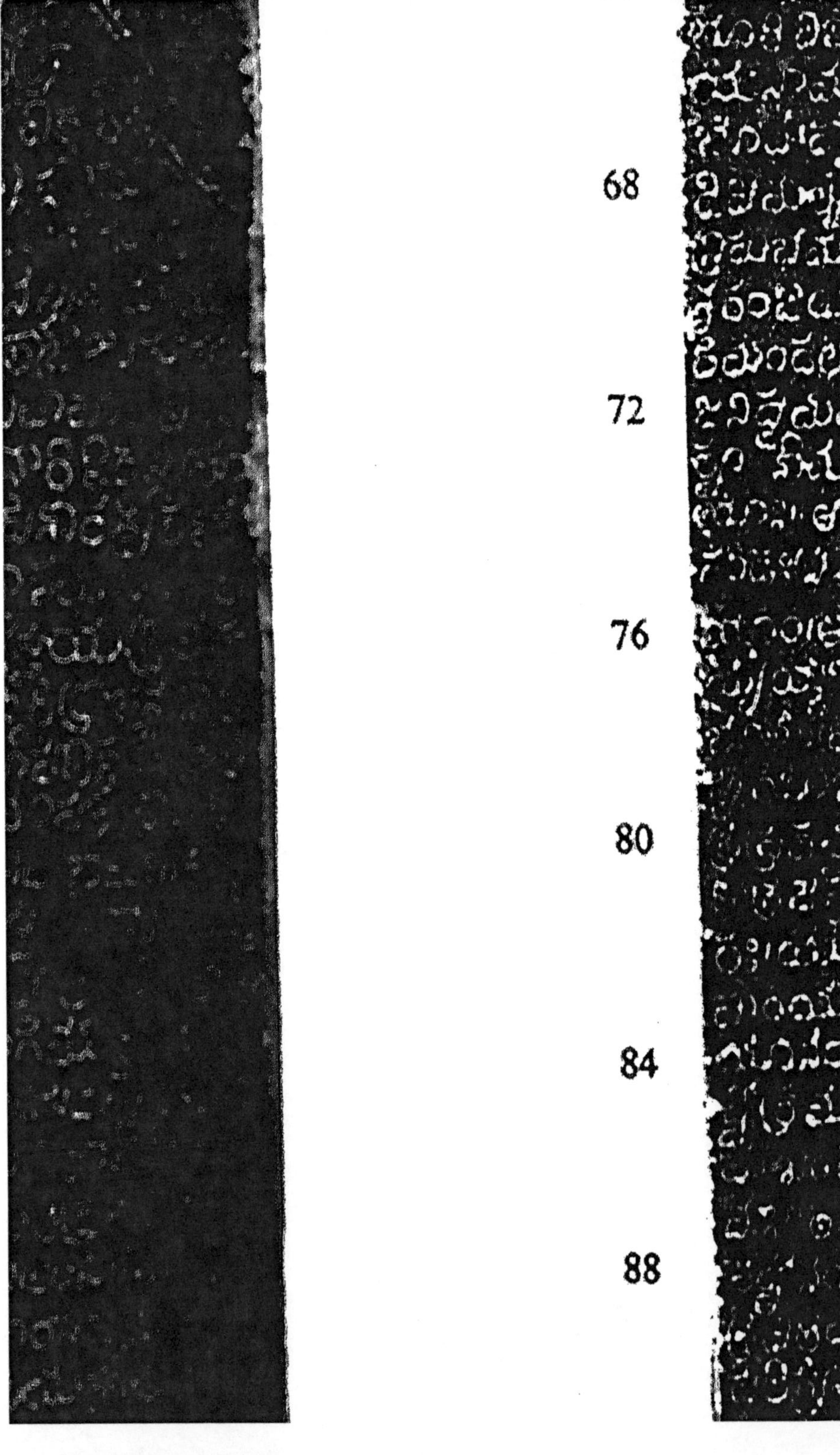

ప్రవాహోథవా ధృతి నిధి దాత్య లతిశ్మ[ద]
తయో న విభాగభాజః॥ గుణై
ః ద్విత్రైః కామం సంతు కులాంగ
ప్రత్యగుణః శ్రీమా నన్వియా దే
॥ శిరః పురారే రివ చంద్రలేఖయా
వ రుచా దివస్థలం । యయోన్న
ఏ మంత్రిణః కులం మనోజ్ఞయా
పయిష్యతే॥ చమూపతే ర్దన్న
మా త్స సబ్బసేనాపతి రుద్ర
క్రాప్రీతస్నేహా దశావలంబా ద్యో
లకుల ప్రదీపః ॥ ఖండయ
న్నః కేవలం మండలాగ్ర మ[న్య -]
క । దండభృద్విపుల విక్రమో[మ్య]
శ్చ నిజస్య రామో మనః॥ తతో

కార్త్తికేయః॥ సుదండనీతిం త

ఁ మమాత్య కృత్యే వృత రుద్రదే

ంషా సంకిసాధీశ వంశవారాశి

రోహిణీవ జనానంద మిందుం వ

ంతీ॥ యస్మి న్నూర్జిత విక్రమే గణ

తే[ః]శాసనా జ్జైతుం దక్షిణ వారి

గా చేలు మ్మణాంసి ద్విషాం। కిం

యోగవేగితచమూయాత్రా

యా ఘూయో ఘూరి పరాశ

రువ్యాణ సమాశంకితః॥ య

ప్రందధాటీ తురగ ఖుర పుటక్షేప ని

ంమే యద్విశై ర్ధూళిజాలై రవిరల మభి

రప్రకాశైః। మా మేష ప్రాప్తరోష క్ష

ః కి న్విరతి వ్యగ్రితో ర్ధి ద్విణపం।పాదా

లబ్ధ్వా జయ్యేతాంసతి సతి । న శిలం క
్య వృత్త మ ప్యన్యవత్తేత॥ ప్రతిష్ఠాభి
గై శ్చ సురా న్యూమి సురా నపి । స
చ్ఛేయతాం శంభో ల్లింగై స్థావర
తిథయః ప్రతిపన్ముఖ్యాః కాల
పి తన్మయః కథితః ॥ ఇతి సర్వ కాల
థ దాన మనేక మదిషాతాం॥ తి
ాత్మా । క్షీరవారాజ్య రూపా స్స
పితాంగా స్వచ్ఛేతాం గాం చ సా
స్ఫుట మితి దశ ధేనూః ప్రార్థ నా[కా]
వ్యేధివ దమల చిత్తా విప్రభక్తా వ
నా త్మైవ కేవలం యాఖ్యా ము[ఖా]
కే కులే । ఉభా చ లోకా విజితా వి
థయతో ముఖః ॥ అగ్రవీర ద్వ

త్ర శృక్షాజలం । అన్నేశ్వరం బలం నష్టః

యాతు నై తేశ్వరం పరం ॥ ప్రాసాద

మథా త్రికూటతుంగం శ్రీశాగ్ని

మహో మహేశలింగం । జ్యోతిర్భిః త్రి

ంభృ నై రశూన్యః శోణిస్థ స్త్రిభు

ంగ్రహో న్యః ॥ ప్రాసాదా గ్రా

దేవళ తమతయా మైలమాంబా

స్నిగ్ధా స్తచ్చిత్రవృత్యా బుధజనమ

సచ్చరితై స్సుచిత్రాః । తస్యా స్తుంగా శ్ర

చరణయుగప్రీతిః పుష్కలా

స్నేహేన భర్తుః స్పృహా విపులదయార్దా

మ్మాహిషః ॥ పరబలభీమకులాశ

రాయగరుడాఖ్యకులభూషా । ఏ

తి మపరా ణ్యాతిష్ఠిప నైమ్మలమాంబ తి

॥ ఏ షైవ మేకవింశత్యా । పతిపాలి । పం

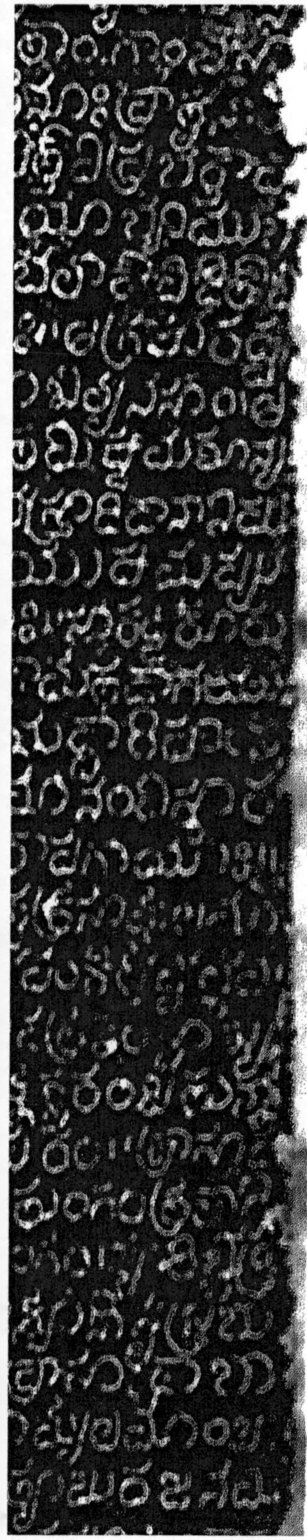

ద్దే దుందుభి నంవత్సర త
్యం। పూర్వ్వజాస్యాం నిజభవనే
తేశ్వరో౽ష్ఠత్॥ య దక్షి ణ భూ
॥ శకాబ్దికా స్తదా పరే దేవ
త్ । సా శ్రైలమాన్నేశ్వర మల్లి
ాకాదికే క్రోధన మా[ఘ]మధ్య
ర్ద్ధేవాంగభోగాయ కాలికాలీని
వ_ర్తనాని వాంఛ్యంతి నంసారా ర్తే
నం॥ మార్గ్గనలిల్యాక నివ ర్తనవింశ
ప్సిశా మది మనోరమ పుష్ప
చంద్రతారకమహోదధి శ్రైలమా
శ్ర విప్రజన సాఙ్క్య(శ్య) లవ త్యసంఖ్యా
త్రాం ద్విజాతిభ్యో యత్నా ద్రక్ష యు
హి మ్మహీశ్వతాం శ్రేష్ఠ దానా చ్ఛ్రే

ం రత్నికా మేకాం భూమే ర
। హార న్నరక మాన్నోతి యా
వం ॥ అకరస్య కరాదా
స్త్రి(ః స్మృ)తః । సకరస్య కర
ఫల మశ్నుతే ॥ స్వదత్తా ద్విగు
త్తానుపాలనాత్ (నమ్) । పరద
త్తం నిష్ఫలం భవేత్ ॥ త
హా త్తవ్యం ధనం దేవద్విజన్మనా
త్తు సకలం లభతే వాంఛి
ఛ్ఛః కృతిచి త్తవ న్నవరసో
శ్రీవ ద్యశ్యాపుయ్యా ఫలప్రద
త్రదానోపమం సాతం శా[ట]
కజలం ప్రాంధా త్తడాగం పు[వ]
భకురస్య దైవతగురు [శ్రీకం]

for the worship and offerings to the gods ar

by Gaṇapatidēva mahārāja is also recorded i

Text

ల సేవకుం శా

షట్ప్రదర్శిమునినా

మూర్తుల నెవ్వడుం బ్రి

సుర కోటికి న్వరదు

కు సుస్థిరస్థితిం గా

త్తిఁ యుగు కాటయ

దల్ ॥ చరణ సరోరు

ల న్మహిష్మని శిరం

ంధ్యా ప్రరుచి నెనయ

గాన్విత దుగ్గిఁ చరము గాట

॥ ఉరగేంద్ర దిగ్గజములకు

కాముగ నాచప్రతము వోలె

శ్మనివాసుండును నైన రుద్రనరేంద్ర మ
నను సదారాధిత త్రినేత్రుండును వి
నవసంతుండును రమణీయ్య సీమ
ంతుండును సకలజనమనోరంజ
నరాతిరాజ మదభంజనుండును శరణా
రణ్యుండును వినుతాఖిలరాజ వరే
ను ధైర్యాజామర సానుమంతుండునుం దు
ుండును సత్యహరిశ్చంద్రుండును
రేంద్రుండును నైన గణపతిదేవ మ
కుం బ్రధానినై ॥క॥ కనకాచలధీరు
వినుతచరిత్రుండు గాయ్యాజావిదుం డినకే
ుండు గుణనిధి కెజ్జమతనయుండు
ాసుతనయుం డనగాంన్ ॥త్రి॥ త్ర
పాలకుంజర మద॥పారంభ నంద

ండును నైన రేచెర్ల రుద్రునకుం బ్రధా
కులతిలకుండు వసుధామరజలధి
ం డశేషజనసుతచరిత్రుం డలఘు
రు దావానలుం డనంగాం బ
నాయకుం డుర్విని ॥ లోక్కేరలోని వీర
వధించి గో[ధు]మశాలిం తలదెంచి
ధించి వడిరాయనిం దోలి దాణా
శ్వర దేవర కతయ దీపంబులు ని
నమేతుం డైన రాజెనాయంకునికి ధర్మ
సుచారిత్రయు వనితాలలామయునైన రవ
సుపుత్రుండు ॥ క ॥ సరనిధిగంభీరుండు
శీలుండు వంశశేఖరుండు దయాక
ధాంబుజదళశతకరుం డని వర్ణింప నో
లయు దాతిని ॥ విశద యశుండైన గణప

ఘ శుద్ధ ౧౫ గురువారము
చలింగాలకూను పింటఅపల్లి
ంహ్మణ ప్రిత్తులు గాక సర్వా నమస్య
చ్చి పెంచెయ్యిన మీంది కాల్వను కొ
క్ష దక్షిణమూను ఆవాంక అడ్డా
మిట్టలూను రవ్వసాని అనకిం
ంతవట్టు గూడను ర్ ౧౩ ॥
ము కాల్వను ర్ ౧ చోలు బాడె కాల్వ
ర్ ౧ కాట్నాయుని చెయ్యిన బ్రాహ్మ
గాక సర్వమాంను రవ్వసాని
రవ్వసాని మామిడితోంట పడమ
రాజెనాయంకుని చెయ్యిన ర్ ౧
ం యేరువాక గుబ్బలి జగదేవ
ణమున ర్ ౨ం దీని దక్షిణము
టిలోన ర్ ౪ం బొమ్మకంటి వెయ్యి వి

va; [A.D. 1246]

tions the king's name and the gods Vaij

TEXT

–

ర వీర

– – వరమ – –

–

– క్రో రాజా

– – శర

శ్వర - -

దే]

లు

బి

౧౧౬౮ వరా

కాత్రిణక

-] వు

_జ

వ్యశ్రీ)

_న

ఋల]

-

-

- తము

ంయకునకు

ార ప్రిత్తి సేసి అయ

లు - - - అపహా

- - -

మగళ

ప్తి ప్తి ప్తి - -

ర - - --

-

ధపి - - -

- వ - - - -

- -

ter is said to have constructed some templ
gifts of lands by others are also recorde
d Ūṭupalli are mentioned.

TEXT

- కా - - -]
క్షో గురుః
శివ ఏ -
గణానామ
రుద్రలోక
మహాదేశి[క -]
మనస్య వా[ ]
మో హానిష్య[- -]
వాత్మనా
ష్టః వరా [-]

ంధ్య కుంకుమ తది ద్య

ా చందనధామో [- -]

స్వహా త్రిభువనత్రయ్యాం[- -]

ర్యతే ।

-

-

ర[ా]గ్య శివాఖ్య శైవముని[రో]

కథానితస్యా[పిం]తః శ్రీమ[త్]

-]ద్రవాసు పరసః పర్యా

నిత్య శ్రీ[శ్రీ]తనివ త్రానా

త్రై షాం సమీపస్థితా

-॥]సహపాల కుంట

త్రి శివా యాదదాతి

నాని విశ్వస్య ధాత్రే

్యరాయ॥ ఊటుపల్లి మ

ంవి మ[లీ]శ్వర శంభ వే।

ఎహో భక్త్యా మైదేవః ప్ర

—

్ఠతి యావ దా

ప్లవం॥ [గిరా] ధమ్మ్ర

్రీ రాజ్ఞో గణప[తే గ్గ]

చ్ఛాసన మిదం య - - -

్ బృహస్పతిః[॥]అనారత

జటినమా[త్రే కృష్ణా]

డక కమండలుం[- -]

రుమహాంభీయు ॥

ు హే సంప్ప

ం దీప్రా౹ తే[–]

ంయుకొ పా౹

ద్వాణసమీహి –

కొ[– – –]బ్ర

[– – – – –]

– –

– –

– – –త్రంయు

రతత్వ సముద్రవే ॥

No. 33

(*A. No. 250 of 1971*)

హారణ - - -]

- ప్రదకా]

గావతార[కద]

. జయ

ణ - - - -

- -

. - -

. - -

. - -

. - -

(శ్రీమ -]

ామంత పల్ల -]

రాజు ప]

- - -]

No. 34

(A. No. 289 of 1968)

౭౦ శివాచార్య్యులు చంద్రవల్లి

- - -] కమ్మ[ము] వల్లి [- -] సేసిన

-] వరకు అంగరంగ భోగాలకై ౧౨

- - - - - ల పెద్దవల్లిగ - ళ -

- - - ర - స్వామి భో

- - ఇ - - ంన - ఖ - ద్గా

- - కుంట [అందున]

ిథ దేవరకు కల [- - - ట]

ముద్రం [- -] కరేగడు భూమి [- -]

దేవరకు మ - - తె

లకు - - - - -

ష్ఠలు ఇ కూ - ంకుల

e main door of the Lakshminārāyaṇa temple
a śu. 7, Thursday [A.D. 1235, May 26; Sa

ivi ?)
characters.
ation [of probably the image of Viśv
med Nārāyaṇa son of Vāmidēva of the Vas

TEXT

के ११५७ युवा संवत्सरे वैसाघ शुध ६
व राज्ये श्रीमहाप्रधान रायस्थापनाचार्य
ई वसिष्ठ गोत्र वामिदेवपुत्र[दादोदै]
T । [धीरो गुणकता - -] गणपतिः
सौ [वर - -] महीमंडली [चंड]कीर्ति
r : त्रिदशगणयुतो[दीवयानुग्रहाथती प्रभ
महा श्री श्री श्री] - - - - -

No. 36

(A. No. 50 of 1971)

HASNABAD

(*A. No. 239 of 1971*)

YELGEDU

(*Peddapally Taluk*)

Provenance not known.

a su. 5, Guru [A. D. 1301, June 27, Thu

:va

f some local taxes like *pannu*, *kānika*, *kaṭ*
ti to the god Rāmanāthadēva by the que
erit of her father Pāldēvanāyinimgāru.

TEXT

ర్గ్రహా

గాక

ర రు

గా

ర

దే

త్రి

ని

క[తీ]

అ త

ంల

ఏదుంది

[దుండు]

ులకు

లేదు ఇం

చంద్రసూ

No. 38

(A. No. 92 of 1970)

CHITTAPUR

(Metpally Taluk)

On a broken stone in the Hanuman *tōṭa*

ıa śu. [Sōma]

dinate named Chinni Rudradēva Mahār
customary. Certain Bairiseṭṭi of the Vırab
iyala included in Chinnapariyala-*stala* the
ıra and Nāgēśvara and endowed them with
akala-*samudra* newly constructed by him.

ర ప్రశస్తి సహితు

స్తి శ్రీ మంన్మహా మం

క కాకతియ్య ప్రతాప

మహారాజులు

వినోదంబు

జ్యంబు సేయు

స్వస్తి శ్రీ జం

సమస్త ప్రశస్తొపే

పంచమహా

పరమేశ్వర అ

కమళ కళికావికా

ప్రథాప లంకేశ్వర

గాభీర హిమ

ఉభయదళ

ంశోౕధ౯వః। (శ్రీ) చింన్నిరు
ుహారాజులు । నాయ
[పి]ంనపరియ్యాల స్తల
పెద్ద పరియ్యాలను॥ స్వస్తి
ువనాఖ్యాత అయ్యా
ాళత వీరసహస్ర సహ
ాలంక్రిత భగవతీలభు
ప్రసాద సత్యశౌచాచా
చారిత్ర నయవినయ
విమళదిగు భరిత
రబలింజ్యధర్మోపదేశ
న శై రిసెట్టింగారు ఉపక్రమ
సిద్ధ త్రికూటము
సకలేశ్వర నాగేశ్వర దేవర॥
సిన సాపాలకు

ఊటుంగాల్వన నీరు

౽నమస్యము మఱుతురు ॥ [-]

ాల్వ [పంకది] ప్రిత్తి పాదుక[ర ।]

ము [చెములవేగిలి] అఱు

ు ర౽ ఋప్పలు ఊరి

పది ౧౦ అస్త్రానాల తూ

కోంట ఒకటి ౧ భైరిసెటింగా

గాృణ ప్రిత్తులు క్రయమూ

౦౦] గోంన్నవి యూఊరనె పెద్ద

వెనుక తూము కాల్వను

ుక్కా మఱుతుఁరు ర[౧]

కోంన వెలివాల

న్న౽పురపు త్రోవను వం

సును [ఏ]ఖండముం గొలచి
మూడను మానెడు ౧ తోక
ండం పది ౧౦ ఆకుల మా [వ]
వెలెడు ౧ నూనెగానుగు
ండిండు ౧ సిద్దెను పోలెడు ౧
వెనుక కొల్చు మఱ్ఱురున
ండు న ౧

లశ్రుతి శ్లోకాలు ॥ సామాన్యో [యం]
సేతున్నృపాణాం కాలేకాలే పాల
భవద్భిః । సబ్బానివాతని [ధా]
పార్థి వేంద్రా భూయో భుయో
తే రామచంద్రః ॥ సదత్తం వ
వా । ఒహారేంత వసుంధరా । షష్టి

No. 39

(*old stock*)

REGONDA

(*Karimnagar Taluk*)

On a stone in the house of the Patel Ra

śva

t of four *marturs* of *chēnu* to the god Sō

TEXT

్రమును]

ండ

ంకతి

్యయుంఘు]

-

ూంద వ

No. 40

(A. No. 345 of 1968)

ADIVISOMANAPALLI

(Manthena Taluk)

Near the cave of Rāmēśvara.

›f 10th century A.D.

pannasa (land-gift) for the offerings, ...
...ukaṁṭi Mucchi Raḍḍi.

TEXT

...]నుకంటి ముచ్చి రడ్డి యీారామీశ్వర
...నకూ దీపానకూ ముగ్గునకూ విడిచిన
...రు దప్పినాను గంగ కఱుత కవిల[పో]
...ను[యింతవట్టు]
... అ
... — వాడు

No. 42

(*A. No. 2 of 1969*)

POLĀVASA

(*Jagtyal Taluk*)

On a pillar near the local Panchayat Office

...obably the day when it was set up as a ...

aiyala. Other details not clear.

TEXT

షణంబులు [౧౨౨౪]
త్సంవత్సర[పుష్య]

–

–

–

మల్యాల – –

–

–

No. 44

(A. No. 23 of 1971)

SANIGARAM

(Karimnagar Taluk)

On a broken stone pillar in front of

aracters of post Kākatīya script. Sanskrit

ళ నవద్రా - - -

హా టీనా

బలభుజబలో

యొన ॥౨౦॥ అ - - -

సుమిత్రా - - -

- ద్ర - - -

- - -

- - -

ం - - -

॥౨౨॥ - - -

న [మంక]

ప్రహేతం కా - -

ం యశో

- - - త

నాయక - - -

ాయ - -

ఁమ్మర్గం - -

దినమణి - - -

త్యతిమనా - -

పియ్యా్య - - -

హారే రాసి - - -

తినాస్యా - - -

. —

. —

- - -

మహి - -

ప్ర - - -

దరే - - -

(*Manthena Taluk*)

ar in the *maṇḍapa* of Muktīśvara temple.

ra śu. 1] [A.D. 1397, Feb. 28]

Sanskrit verse in *Śārdūlavikrīḍita* metre ar
ing the festival of *digvijaya* (conquest of the
ari) made the gift of *Tulāpurusha* on Wedn
f the sixteen *mahādānas* (noble charities)
and generally performed by royal digni
that of the donor.

Text

ం[ద్ర]* విశ్వగణితే శ్రీగౌ[తమీ]

ఈశ్వర వత్సరాదిమది[నే]

కృతీ। కుర్వాన్ దిగ్విజయో

శ్రీదేవరాయో నృపః శ్రీ[ము]

ధన్యమహిమా దానం తులాపూ

కృష్ణనామప్రభుః। శ్రీనారాయణ పదచి
। సంసారయోగీ[మతః] ।౧। యం [ద్గురి
ప్రధిధగుణగణో రామనామా యశ [స్వి]
లఖయాఖ్యో[విలి]ఖత చరిత క్రిష్ణ [మా]
౹ తఖ్యాస్తం రామక్రిష్ణం విమళ - -
త్ర కృష్ణో మహోయ్యాణః
సదమ పదపరో విష్ణు భక్తి - -
ంతగిరి నాథస్య [రం]తుం లక్ష్మి స[మ]
చ - - -
కం॥ శాలివాహాన [శా] కానాం
చ[శధుః]శతం । త్రింశ[త - -]
ప] యాశ్వరే మాసి మాధవే । [శుక్ల ద]
ౠ]చ। నిమఋతం విష్ణు [మందిరం]
కృష్ణో[-] రామపరః । యశో

ain Tummikhāṃ built the entrance gate (
le towards its expenses.

TEXT

-]

[రం- - -]

ందు[- -]

ి కటించి[- -]

ుందుకు [ఱ]

గాంతరంపా - - -]

No. 48

(*A. No. 558 of 1968*)

VELLULLA

(*Metpalli Taluk*)

On a slab set up in the sluice of the tanl
... 5 Thursday [A.D. 1613, April

చ్చెను శ్రీ శ్రీ శ్రీం వేయునూ !

No. 49

(*A. No. 42 of 1971*)

DHARMAPURI

(*Jagtyal Taluk*)

ι pillar of the *maṇḍapa* in the Brahmapu

va, Vaiśākha śu. 13, Sōmavāra [A. D. 1

rāya.

onstruction by certain Tirmalaya son of
e *Pushkaraṇi* and the *maṇḍapa* on th
alli Dharmāraya. The latter is also state

TEXT

సిం

గ

ు

్రాశ

ాపనం

ం బాధ

్రాయ

్త పుస్త

ట్టు

ులు

ుమ పే

టుం

ుతా

No. 51

(*A. No. 559 of 1968*)

VELLULLA

(*Metpalli Taluk*)

a boulder by the side of the Hanuman in

[A. D. 1665]

No. 52

(*A. No. 97 of 1971*)

MANIPALEM

(*Huzurabad Taluk*)

On a stone slab containing the image of Ha

Māgha śu. 10 Guruvāra [A. D. 1756]

illegible.

aph was set up by certain Venkatarāya
lear.

TEXT

భ్యుదయ శాలివా

ములు ౧౬౭౮ [నాంటి] యు

ర మాఘ శు॥ ౧౦

గాండు [మాదాలి గా]

is intended for growing a flower garden fo

TEXT

ాభ్యుదయ ప్రవర్తమాన శాలివాహాన

... । అగు నేడు భావనామ సమ్వర మా...

నాడు రాజశ్రీ జుపూ[డి] ధర్మారావు దేశ...

మ్మడి వెంన్నఅయ్య[కి] వ్రాశియిచ్చిన భూదాన

ంగల సాలు [తు]॥ తింర్మలాపురంలోను శ్రీ

వ్వులవనం వేశి అం [దుక్కపొలంయీ]వలెనని

[గెయీగ్గుండుఙాల] బుట్టిగడు [విజబొ]న...

కుంచాల వడ్ల పడుఖాటు పొలం నీకు[యి...

అగ్గున ఏండాదిన నులతోటం పువ్వుల [వనం

]పూల పూజ చేస్తూ వుండి అందుకు యిత్తి

త్ర పారంపర్యాయమున్ను దేవుని పూజ

విన పలం అనుభవించి(ది నుయును। మితికా

āvaṇa, (Sna. 1070)

shāh.

g to the *farman* of the Sultan, his officer,
ld coins to the Havaldar Menāvi Beg for

TEXT

ంర్యాను కల్గుంచ్చి
వ౯ాన్నుౕలు ౫౮ం
సమాను సి
అలపున్న ౧౦౩[౦]
ంహ్మా తేత్ర
కేవ బ్రాంహ్మణ
త్తులు యు
ంలవె యవ్వ
ంత్యం చేసి
్యంచ్చవలెను
విజీథవ
యుతు
గాం

No. 55

(*A. No. 133 of 1970*)

SIRCILLA

(*Sircilla Taluk*)

...iva *saṁvatsara*.

TEXT

... సంవ్వత్సర అ

... - - బోనల

... - - - - వివ

... - ద్రక్శ

-

No. 57

(*A. No. 95 of 1971*)

KAMALAPUR

(*Huzurabad Taluk*)

On a stone set up in the floor near the Ś...

...cters.

...ha ba. 6 Gu.

... gift made by Jūpalli Raṁgapati Dhar(m)...

ont of the *garbha-griha* of the Śrīrāma te

f certain Kānula Anantu's son, Gaurayya's

TEXT

ా॥

ని శే ॥

'మూరు

ర్య[మూ]

౦ ।ని। కోమూ

। నిర్య

No. 59

(A. No. 47 of 1971)

No. 60

(*A. No. 287 of 1968*)

KASIPETA

(*Manthena Taluk*)

On a pillar in the *mukhamaṇḍapa* of th

:it, Āshāḍha śu. 12, Śanivāra (Saturday)

rtion not clear.

Kottakoṁḍḍa sīma, Muttanūru village a

TEXT

తు నామ

ర ఆషాఢ శు॥

వారంనాడు

ంఢ్ల శీమలో

No. 62

(*A. No. 130 of 1971*)

KONAPUR

(*Jagtyal Taluk*)

On a stone near the Āñjanēya temple.

the 15th century

śu. 14, Guruvāra (Thursday)

d to certain Sārvabhūmuni Narusaya b

TEXT

te

ation certain devotees.

TEXT

కక గుణగణాలం[క్రిత] సత్య

ా[ర] శ్రీ [-]* స [మ్మన్నస్వ-]

చ్చి[ష్య - - - -]

స్ బ్రాహ్మణభక్త (శ్రీ) [మతు]

No. 64

(*A.No. 95 of 1970*)

GAMBHIRPUR

(*Metpalli Taluk*)

On the foot steps of the Venkate

rn Telugu characters - abraded.

not clear.

BHUSHANRAOPET

(*Metpalli Taluk*)

On a stone in the patel's fi

Jaina image at the top.

and illegible.

t clear.

TEXT

[ಕಂಯುವ]

— —

) — —

— — —

No. 66

(*A. No. 5 of 1967*)

POLASA

(*Jagtyal Taluk*)

certain devotee, name not clear, who was th

TEXT

—]

S

No. 68

(*A. No. 90 of 1971*)

RAIKAL

the construction of the fort of Pratāpagiri
vattu gaṇḍa, *Gaṇḍa gōpāla*, *Kāṁchi raksha*
yagajakēsari, *arirāya-gaja-kēsari* and *Telug*

TEXT

ంవత్సర [వు] శాఖ శు 3 వ

ండ్డ [గో పాళ] ? కాంచ్చి రక్షపా

ాపనాచాయ్యౄ [పా] ండ్యమను విభాళ

ర। దాయగ [జ] కేసరి। అరిరాయగ

ంగురాయ — —

ప్రనాయునింగారు ప్రతాపగిరి

ఆచంద్రాకౄ [మవు]

ష్టించ్చిరి మంగళమహా

శ్రీ శ్రీ యును.

No. 70

(*A. No. 3 of 1972*)

KALESVARAM

(*Manthena Taluk*)

(... ... ...)

KALESVARAM

(*Manthena Taluk*)

On the *dhvajastambha*.

. 10, Sōmavāra

In character of 16th-17th centuries

of the Nandi-pillar by certain Baloju son

TEXT

సంవత్సర చై

[నో] [ము] తినాధని

[తిడురో] జు పు

రోజు నందికం

ంచెను శ్రీ శ్రీ

No. 72

ILLINTHAKUNTA
(*Huzurabad Ṭaluk*)

In the maṇḍapa of Surama temple.

Guruvāra

on of the *maṇḍapa* for Yāgaśāla (for per
sister of Bōgam Balarāya.

TEXT

on 8

of certain Nārappati, after striking (

ాము

ండిచి

॥

. On another hero stone at the same pla

of a certain hero named Saṁgama st
Śrīmat Mahā Domerāju.

ాము

ర్గణతో ల్లక

రిలిచ

ి

ేలు

వర

రజా జ

ఇ

గలి

No. 75

(*A. No. 1 of 1969*)

POLASA

(*Jagtyal Taluk*)

On a stone in the Pulastyēśvara temple.

[A. D. 1108]; date not verifiable.

; but Dakshiṇāyana - *sankrānti* stated in th

cription of Pulastyāśrama and the town

the titles of *Lattalūr-puravarēśvara*, *Suvar*

va-divya-śrīpāda-padmārādhaka, and *Śrī*

ం పూర్వ్వదొ ళంధ్రదేశవెసెగు[నీవం]
హం॥ ఆదేశదొళు॥ మనెమనెగత్త [-]
న్యచయం నిధియుంపయంగ ళామన్
యు గ్వరుణియ స్వరియగ్గుణిళు గ్రి
నసిజరూప రంన్వితరుధార లెనలు
ట్టణ జనమత[వాదు]దింద్రన బలీంద్ర
గళొళు॥ ఆ పట్టణదొళు వైరి
నరసుగెయ్యుత్తి[ద్దై],నూప
పతి దామాయమాన[చా]
స్వస్తి సమధిగత పంచమహా
శ్వరం లత్తలూ ప్పురవరాధీశ్వరం
ధ్వజ। మూర్త్తి మకరధ్వజ।
ణ। గుణమణివిభూష
వజ్రప్రాకార। గండరహీర।

೧ ೮.೭ [ ]

ವೀರಲಕ್ಷ್ಮ್ಯಾಲಿಂಗಿ

ಭುವನಪರಾಕ್ರಮೋ[ನ್ನ ತ]ಾ

ಶಿಖಭದ್ರ ವಂಶೋದ್ಭವರಪ್ಪ ಶ್ರೀ

ಮ್ಮಾನ್ನಪ್ವಾ ಸ್ವಾಮಿಗಳುಂ ಮೂವ

ಮುರಿದಂಡಮುಂ ಸಮಸ್ತೋಭ

ಪುಲಸ್ತ್ಯಾಶ್ರಮ ಪಟ್ಟಣದೆ[ಪೆಂ]

ಮಹಾನಾಡಾ ಗಿ[ರ್ದು] ಸಮುದ್ರ

ಿರಿ ಸಂವತ್ಸರದ ಪುಷ್ಯ ಬಹು

ದಕ್ಷಿಣಾಯನ ಸಂಕ್ರಾ[ಂ]ತಿ

ಸ್ತೀಶ್ವರ ದೇವರ ಪರಿಸೂತ್ರಕ್ಕೆ

[ದೆ] ಎತ್ತಿನ ಹೊಲಿಂಗೆ ಪಸವಾಂ

ಹೊಲಿಂಗೆ ವಸವಾಂದು ಸರ್ವಾಯಹ ಸು

ದು ಕ್ಷೇತ್ರಯ

లూ]

కిత ధ్వ

ాయ]

మం

-

[దివ్య]

మరా

న - -

‘

త్ర

ర(?)

ళ బిట్ట

-

త్త

వ [రు]

the *mukhamaṇḍapa* of the Śrīrāma temp

y certain Pariki on the fifth day of Jyēsl

TEXT

———

iddle of their extreme left side edges.

ment is southern Nāgari of the thirtee
, whereas the portion containing the n
gu prose written in Nāgari characters.

in the village Neḍhavūra, when Ravidat
Maṁchi-rāja the minister of Jāyapanāy
instance in the month of Kārtika for
luva of Chāmanapalli, invited the elders c
li, assembled them near the canal and
according to the old arrangement the G
aṅchirāja along with some brāhmaṇas
on his findings to the king). With th
Akayachandradēva (two officers named)
ne to the village (Chāmanapalli) keepin
lēva, and Hingadēva, (the elders) Dāmay
?] (re-examined the case) and taking ev
right on Gonugu-*kāluva* to those brāhm
stood as witnesses.

Text

First Plate : First Side

र्षं ०००[3]०[3] पराभवसंवत्सर पौष्यशु

I PLATE : I SIDE

II PLATE : I SIDE

अप्पय पोंचिराज वोल्लमराज कारपाक र
चवन [प]* ल्लि व्रित्ति ब्रह्मणैश्च विचा
त् पुनश्च गोनुगु कालुवा दत्ता [।।*] अ
- - - - रेंडि] पुराणमु मल्लय सोमेदुल म
- - -] केंकय विंटि मल्ले वेंगिनदेव रे

SECOND PLATE : FIRST SIDE

मनु [त्प - -] मल्लयप्रभृतयो वेणिजः ।
म्मे मंचेकंकि रेंडि विरिद्गल मादेवि [मंच
चुल प्रभृतयः कुटुंबिनः ।। क ।। चामनप
र्थमै अक्षयचंडनिवारु चामेनपल्लि महा
ामालवारि साक्षिगोरिननु कुंमरिकुंटल
न्नि दावनि ना[मि] नायुडुनु रवप कर्सा
कोडुकु मल्लजीयानु मंगड मल्लाडु देवनप
ा [मि] ट्टपल्लि मदिरेड्डिनि गट्लवेल्लि न
[मंग - -] चिसेटिनि मासकम्म मैलिपेद्दि

SECOND PLATE : SECOND SIDE

ce ; *Q.*=Queen ; *Kāsnį.*=Kāsnįrakūṭa,
sec.=sect ; *sect.*=sectarian ; *scr.*=scrib
; *tn.*= town ; *ter.*=term ; *tit.*= title ;
hāļukya ; *Vij.* = Vijayanagar dynasty;

.. .. 15.00

Pradesh :

.. .. 10.00

handra :

.. .. 1.50

Allchin .. 10.00

dhra Pradesh

.. .. 15.00

S. *Gopala-*

.. .. 4.00

of Vishnu-

:

D. .. 3.00

dhra

.. .. 5.00

Pradesh

Rama Rao .. 5.00

dhra Pradesh

Rama Rao .. 3.50

Gopala-

.. .. 14.00

Andhra

.. .. 2.50

Excavations :

S. (Lond.) 20.00

22. A Catalogue of
Edt. by Sri P.V.

23. The Temples of
Dr. M. Rama R

24. Medieval History
Sri S. K. Sinha,

25. A Monograph o
Paintings at Alla
Md. Abdul Wah

26. Bouddha Darsan
Sri K. Lakshman

27. A Monograph o
Kesanapally:
Md. Abdul Wah

28. Copper Plate Ins
State Museum,

29. Studies in Medi
Dr. N. Ramesan

30. Select Andhra T

31. Select Epigraph
Sri P. V. Parabr

32. Corpus of Inscr
Districts, Part
Sri M. Somasek

33. Krishnadevaraya

.. — 6.00

Pradesh Governm

Dr. Parameswaril

eum:

11. Gold and Silver (

D. ... 3.00

Abdul Wali Khan

Epigraphy Series

6. Epigraphia Andl

965 .. 5.50

Edt. by Dr. N. V

V.P. Sastry .. 2.50

Sri P. V. Parabra

n of

n — 2.00

7. Inscriptions of A

District (Under

.. 11.00

by Dr. Venkatara

8. Epigraphia Andh

ah ... 15.00

Edt. by P. V. Pa

Miscellaneous

...

(The Indus People

Parts I-IV) :

Edt. by Dr. R. S

(1972) .. 14.00

(1972 - 1973)

esearch

3. History of Mediev

Edt. by Prof. H. I

of the Books Published Prior to

CPSIA information can be obtained
at www.ICGtesting.com
Printed in the USA
LVOW12s1338050416
482252LV00001B/34/P

9 781846 648113